Thatcher & Apartheid: A Case Study in Conflict

Kurt Messick

Land's End Press - Lubec, Maine

ISBN: 1727021762
ISBN-13: 978-1727021769

DEDICATION

To my dear friend, Anabel Newman, who got to read the draft, but passed away before the final copy, without whose encouragement and support over the years, this (and much else in my life) would not have been possible.

CONTENTS

ACKNOWLEDGMENTS

I wish to thank my friends and supporters through the research and writing process. They include, but are not limited to, Karen Gail Hand, Mark Bond, and Carol Pollio, colleagues of mine from my faculty days with APUS, who provided much needed support and cheerleading, as well as reading and commenting near the end. I also want to thank my friend, Orion Day, for his support and honest critique of my efforts in this writing.

Finally, I want to thank beyond measure my friends at the Ivy Tech Community College Library, and in particular Eleanor Moss, without whose able research and Interlibrary Loan efforts on my behalf over several months, this book would not exist.

1 INTRODUCTION

In Charles Moore's authorized biography of Margaret Thatcher, he stated, with regard to Thatcher's South Africa policies, "Certainly, in the annals of normal diplomacy, this was no way to behave." (Moore 2016, 584) The role of British foreign policy with regard to South Africa during Thatcher's years was controversial to the point that the press, foreign countries in various alliances, and even Thatcher's own cabinet colleagues were in conflict and quandary over how to proceed. By Thatcher's time, Britain's role on the world stage was greatly reduced. In South Africa, however, Britain was still a principle power, with economic and historic ties greater than most if not all other nations. Therefore, Britain's refusal to participate in the communal actions against the apartheid-enforcing South African regime was significant enough to create many conflicts, in domestic politics as well as international affairs. Thatcher found some support early from the much-vaunted special relationship with the United States, which most likely relied heavily on the personal affinities she had with President Reagan. Even that support began to falter as US domestic politics led Congress to chip away at Reagan's resistance to sanctions. There was a difference in the handling of South Africa later in Thatcher's tenure from what had been done in a neighboring country, Rhodesia, early in her first term as Prime Minister. Despite the fact that South Africa went on to relatively successful post-apartheid structure of government and society, can that be said to have been helped or delayed by British actions and inactions during Thatcher's time in office?

This book will explore the development of Thatcher's policies toward South Africa and how they progressed, including with regard to the Commonwealth, the United States, the European Community, and outside nations. Also, how much was owed to Thatcher's personal political philosophies and personal biases will be discussed. Some comparison and contrast with other conflicts Thatcher dealt with will serve as examples of success or failure in terms of consistency and effectiveness. Thatcher was not a lone actor on the world stage, but as Britain had significant, perhaps outsized, influence on South Africa, and Thatcher was a strong leader both in terms of party and policy, she bore much of the responsibility. What role did Margaret Thatcher play in the ending of apartheid in South Africa? Was her action with regard to South Africa consistent with the rest of her foreign policy philosophy? Was her action effective in terms of continuing engagement and bringing about change in South Africa, which was the goal of the international pressure being brought by others?

2 THEORETICAL FRAMEWORK

This book uses an historical case study approach, defined by Theis (2002) as "based on a selective, critical reading of sources that synthesizes particular bits of information into a narrative description or analysis of a subject." (352) This will include to the extent possible in the given parameters of time and resources archival research, content analysis and interviews.

Much has been published in terms of policy papers, speeches, and government papers regarding the actions and interactions of the principal actors as well as how they were viewed from the outside. Some work contains basic information – statements of fact relatively free from interpretation (Thies

2002, 353). However, even official policy statements falter due to issues of interpretation and implementation, as well as follow-up statements and actions which may be contradictory. The issue of apartheid and South Africa, and in particular Margaret Thatcher's role in dealing with the issue, had significant press coverage, which shall also be explored.

In a case study, interviews would be ideal, but given the passage of time, many of the key actors have passed away, or are for practical purposes not readily accessible. Both Margaret Thatcher and Nelson Mandela passed away in the same year. However, many of the key actors produced memoirs, autobiographies, and published collections of speeches and writings that can serve some of the aspects of this part of the study. This will often require an awareness of bias on multiple levels.

While it seemed to many that South Africa was a singular case, looking at this case, both in terms of the particular actor involved (Thatcher) as well as the broader issues (effectiveness of methods), one might draw some parallels to other nations and international situations where particular actors and particular regimes might fit part of the case model here. Also, is it necessarily the case that much or all is dependent upon the particular actor? When dealing with intractable problems, such as apartheid in South Africa over several decades, and leaders who are have a reputation for difficulty, knowing cases from the past can help in planning strategy or avoiding pitfalls in the future. According to Pal (2005), "cases are sometimes thought to be instances of more general phenomena, not necessarily in a statistically representative sense, but more as exemplars." (229)

3 LITERATURE REVIEW

Approaching this topic as a case study in conflict, and Thatcher's role in the conflict in particular, there are many types of literature available to address the issue from different points of view.

Primary Sources

The Parliamentary Record, *Hansard*, is useful in terms of the Parliamentary debates, question time queries and responses, policy statements read in the chambers, petitions and divisions. Extensively available online and searchable, it provides a verbatim account of what Thatcher and other Ministers, Members and Lords actually said in the Chambers. Of particular use are questions and answers from Question Time.

Another source of primary material is contained in the archives of the Margaret Thatcher Foundation, which includes much of the Hansard material, but goes further to include outside speeches, letters, interviews and other statements. The site also contains commentary and journalism collected over time about Thatcher, which includes her involvement with South Africa; these sources will be regarded in a different fashion from the primary material.

Robin Harris has edited a volume of Thatcher's speeches, which also serves as primary material. This book is more of a "highlights" than a comprehensive collection. It contains fifty-seven key speeches during her career, with side commentary by Harris, which again will be counted separately from primary material. The issue of South Africa arises three times in this collection of fifty-seven speeches, from her early premiership to one speech given well past her resignation and the end of apartheid.

Primary material from other political figures in

Britain comes from Foreign and Commonwealth Office archives. Speeches, letters, and other statements from South African figures, including Mandela, de Klerk, P.W. Botha and Pik Botha, among others, are often contained in historical archives online, which will be useful.

Memoirs and Autobiographies

Much of the literature includes memoirs, autobiographies and authorized biographies that will naturally be biased toward what the principal author wants presented, both in terms of content and personal interpretation. Use of overlapping sources will help mitigate the bias. Other literature contains political, policy and personal history that by its very nature will be susceptible to bias and revision, and can range from the hagiographic to the scathing indictment, particularly when there is a figure like Margaret Thatcher involved. Including the different perspectives can give a fuller sense of the issues. Thatcher's own autobiography, along with the recent authorized biography by Moore, are included, as are works by other British officials (government, party, and FCO), South African leaders on various sides, and outside figures who also played a role in the policies or actions.

Thatcher's own two-volume autobiography includes her take on the South African situation at different points in her political career, but it is all given with the value of hindsight, and a reasonably successful and peaceful resolution to the apartheid situation. This is also true of Geoffrey Howe's memoirs, which include not only the value of hindsight in this regard, but also the aftermath of his painful role in government, both with his own resignation and his role in forcing Thatcher's resignation.

The autobiographies, memoirs and biographies of South African figures such as Nelson Mandela, F.W. de Klerk, Pik Botha and others often treat Thatcher less extensively, but their responses at the time and commentaries after serve to show different ways in which her actions were perceived. Mandela in particular was known to be magnanimous during the struggle and in victory; his statement regarding Margaret Thatcher that "we have much to be thankful to her for," is often interpreted in this way (BBC interview, margaretthatcher.org).

Histories

There are many histories that are available on overlapping subjects: history of British foreign policy in the twentieth century, history of British political involvement in Africa post-World War II, history of apartheid, history of South Africa, and more. For purposes of this paper, general history will be less useful, but histories that deal with the British foreign policy toward South Africa with regard to the apartheid issue as well as those that look at the final decade of apartheid, which overlaps mostly with Thatcher's tenure as Prime Minister, are useful.

Barber and Hill's book, *The Uneasy Relationship Britain and South Africa,* is useful in that it was written just as Thatcher's time as Prime Minister began. At this point, Rhodesia was still an issue, and the changing nature of Britain's role in the world as well as Britain's role with Africa generally, and South Africa in particular, were beginning to be more apparent and influential in government policy and public understanding. As Barber states in his introduction, Britain's general response took one of three forms, a conservative, a radical and a middle-road liberal approach, the latter of which was more popularly expressed: "The public debate in Britain is largely conducted in liberal terms, with widespread condemnation of apartheid, but little support for revolutionary change. Peaceful reform is most favoured and that is the position generally adopted by the government." (Barber and Hill 1983, 6)

Hyam and Henshaw's *The Lion and the Springbok* gives a broad overview of the history of relations between Britain and South Africa from the Boer War to South Africa's departure from the Commonwealth. The final chapter, however, is perhaps most important here, as it covers the post-World War II period through to 1994 with speculations on the future of South Africa's relationship with Britain and the Commonwealth in a post-apartheid environment. Beinart's *Twentieth-Century South Africa* and Clark and Worger's *South Africa: The Rise and Fall of Apartheid* cover the subject of South Africa and apartheid without a particular view toward Britain or Thatcher, but are useful in that it thus helps demonstrate how important the relationship is. The historical record is mixed in terms of the effectiveness of sanctions, particularly under Botha, but almost all agree that Thatcher's style and tone was a contentious issue apart from the practical policy of general economic sanctions.

Journalism

Journalistic literature often lacks the later perspective available to writers who can take the more historical view, but does serve to show the in situ sense of the problems. Again the question of bias comes up, particularly dealing with British newspapers of the period of Thatcher's tenure of office. In particular, the major British newspapers of the time – *The Times, The Telegraph, The Independent, The Guardian* – as well as some of the tabloid press have articles that express opinions and bias as well as information. Even those parts of the press that tended toward being Tory supporters would often part company, at least somewhat, over this issue. Included in the heading of journalism are periodicals such as *The Economist* and *Foreign Affairs*, both of which have a number of articles dating from the late 1970s to the early 1990s useful for seeing how Thatcher and

Britain were being perceived at the time.

Commentaries and Outliers

Beyond this, an example of something a bit outside the above categories would be Filby's *God & Mrs Thatcher,* which contains a section on South Africa that highlights yet another type of literature, that works to go beyond the political and personal. Filby traces South Africa as in part a spiritual struggle, aided by the Anglican church, itself an institution with interesting intersections in policy implications, and other international organizations.

There are also reflections and commentaries by actors involved in the issue, such as Carrington, Renwick, Cradock, and Fraser. Berlinski's book, *There is No Alternative: Why Margaret Thatcher Matters* and Brown's book, *The Myth of the Strong Leader: Political Leadership in the Modern Age* provide insights into the general character of how Thatcher approaches conflict. Books specific to the issue of social conflict and conflict resolution, such as those by Pruitt and Kim's *Social Conflict: Escalation, Stalemate, and Settlement* and .Ramsbotham, Woodhouse, and Miall's

Contemporary Conflict Resolution: The Prevention, Management and Transformation of Deadly Conflicts help round out the discussion by addressing conflicts more generally, and providing some theoretical and other case study insights.

4 THATCHER AND APARTHEID

As her official biographer states, "Mrs Thatcher was accused at home and abroad of being a sympathizer with apartheid." (Moore 2016, 544) However, the reality of the situation was much more complex, and from her own statements as well as those around her, she had no tolerance for it. "Margaret Thatcher is often cast as an apologist for apartheid, although her position on South Africa was complex, pragmatic and, some might argue, a continuation of the British government's position from the 1960s." (Filby 2015, 292) In many ways, Thatcher's actual policies were not unique to her. She was part of a succession of governments, Conservative and Labour, that dealt with the issue of South Africa. Apartheid was not the only issue involved, but it came to be the central focus in the press. "The search for a single overriding objective in Britain's relations with South Africa is a false one." (Barber and Hill 1983, 91)

There was little question that Thatcher did not approve of apartheid. Beyond the racial element, it chaffed against her ideas of freedom and free markets. "She saw the apartheid laws as inhuman and absurd, understanding very well that the people they alienated most were the entire black elite on which the future of the country depended." (Renwick 2013, 183) She believed that the growth, via capitalism, of a black middle class would solve the problem of apartheid without the need for outside intervention or internal revolution.

Thatcher's distaste for apartheid also extended to general demeanor of how South Africa conducted itself more generally. But this was not enough to push her into a course of action she felt strategically and morally unacceptable. "If she had little tolerance for the conduct of the South African regime, however, Thatcher had even less for the idea of imposing more sanctions on it and none at all for pressure on her to do so." (Sharp, 1997, 229) Thatcher's reputation as the Iron Lady, given first with regard to dealings with the Soviet Union, came to also be recognized in many of her foreign policies and attitudes elsewhere. "Thatcher's toughness was conspicuously displayed in the continuing dispute over the Union of South Africa." (Reitan 2003, 115) Riddle (1991) described this as one of "the classic examples of her distinctive, and abrasive, approaches" along with the Falklands and Hong Kong.

5 BRITAIN AND SOUTH AFRICA

In her autobiography, Thatcher wrote, "It would have been better if we had kept South Africa inside the Commonwealth, where we could have influenced her more effectively." (Thatcher 1993, 502) This might have been wishful thinking, and was a perpetuation of the "entrenched belief that Britain has a special role to play in southern Africa." (Barber, in Byrd, 1988, 100) Vinen (2009) states that this was at the time "the area of the world in which the legacies of the British Empire still mattered most." (221) According to Clark and Worger (2016), the creation of South Africa came from the aftermath of the Boer War, was primarily a struggle of gold, and involved a heavy toll in human life due to Lord Kitchener's willingness to bring conflict to civilians. (15) The primary concern after the Boer War was the maintenance of an English-speaking and British-leaning government capable of keeping the Boers at bay. (Tinker 1977) Darwinian ideas of racial superiority were imported and enforced in the area by the likes of Cecil Rhodes and Paul Kruger, but this was not sufficiently distasteful at the time for the British government, or most European governments, to be concerned about. "In 1917 Lloyd George actually convened an Imperial War Cabinet of prime ministers to assist the Cabinet of the mother country. A powerful empire statesman like General Jan Smuts of South Africa was even called upon to participate in the deliberations of the British Cabinet." (Morgan 2005, 103)[1]

Through World War I and World War II, South Africa provided support for the war effort on behalf of Britain, but after the latter war, the international situation had changed sufficiently that Britain's power was lessened, while superpower and

---

[1] It is indicative of the closeness of the British with the South Africans over time that one of two foreign figures remembered in statuary on Parliament Square in London is Smuts; it is perhaps ironic that the other foreign figure included is American President Abraham Lincoln, who freed the African-American slaves.

international organization power and influence grew. "After the Second World War, black expectations of international support shifted to the United Nations, the Organization of African Unity (OAU) and individual black states. However, something of the old hopes of support from Britain persisted." (Barber and Hill 1983, 2) In 1948, South African elections returned an Afrikaner government that continued in the emerging Commonwealth until 1961. (Reitan, 2003, 115)

Apartheid itself was an evolving situation, gaining steam under the Afrikaner government. According to Clark and Worger (2016), the early days of the Union of South Africa saw various efforts back and forth at exclusion and inclusion, but the 1948 victory of the National Party (the Afrikaners) set the stage for the rest of the life of apartheid. "Despite NP ambiguity in defining apartheid, the legislative programming advanced from 1948 through to the 1980s was breathtaking. Every aspect of South African life was determined under law by race." (Clark & Worger 2016, 46) Protests were frequent, and just as frequently put down. Coloured, Indians and Blacks were defined as different groups. So-called grand apartheid (a complete separation of the races) never became economically or socially possible, which was of concern to the white minority in power from the time of Vorwoerd forward. As such, this set the stage for what Edward Azar would classify as a protracted social conflict, in which "the prolonged and often violent struggle by communal groups for such basic needs as security, recognition and acceptance, fair access to political institutions and economic participation." (Ramsbotham 2009, 84)

After the declaration of independence as a republic, South Africa was required to reapply for admission to the Commonwealth. Leaders in the Commonwealth such as Nehru insisted as price of admission the dismantling of apartheid. "Multi-racialism was the keynote of Commonwealth politics during the 1950s and 1960s when the successful adaptation from Empire to Commonwealth was made." (Tinker 1977, 67) However, Premier H.F. Verwoerd of South Africa would not accept this, saying "that to accept an ultimatum from other states on internal policies was inconsistent with independence; hence, his country would withdraw from the Commonwealth." (Tinker, 1977, 68) However, being outside the Commonwealth at that time wasn't a critical blow to an economically strong nation such as a South Africa. Verwoerd said, "South Africa would retain the economic substance of the Commonwealth connection even if it had so clearly rejected the spirit of the multi-racial association." (Hyam and Henshaw 2007, 145)

The economic power of South Africa continued even into the subsequent decades as apartheid became an increasingly problematic factor in foreign relations. "Many of the region's black states which are land-locked had been forced to rely increasingly on South Africa as other routes had closed because of civil war, inefficiency and lack of resources." (Barber 1988, 115) The geography and natural resources of South Africa made them natural, if tense, trading partners with neighbors as well as others who might benefit from cheaper prices from South African sources. "The fact that many African regimes were prepared to meet and do business with South Africa provided it was kept quiet only aggravated South African condescension toward black Africa. The South Africans were no more at home dealing with Western nations. Theirs was a true pariah politik." (Crocker 1994, 33)

The British also maintained strong connections with South Africa, trade-wise. At the beginning of Thatcher's time as Prime Minister, a full ten percent of British overseas investment was in South Africa. "Perhaps the South African remnant of the British economic world system was so durable, or the vision of a post-apartheid South Africa allied to the West so alluring, that the British government could not bring itself finally to terminate the remains of economic connections which had endured since the nineteenth century." (Hyam and Henshaw 2007, 145) Even with minor sanctions and an end to military sales, the percentage of trade between the two nations remained high for both. South Africa's London embassy is their largest abroad, and as many as 800,000 residents in South Africa could claim British citizenship during the last quarter of the twentieth century. (Barber 1988, 98)

6 BRITISH RESPONSES BEFORE THATCHER

In 1960, Harold Macmillan made a famous speech in Cape Town, nicknamed the "winds of change" speech. Included in this speech was the idea that the transition from Empire to Commonwealth had been accomplished. (Otte 2003, 23) However, looking forward, he spoke to his audience, stating that he was "against the emerging British consumer boycott of South African goods, stating towards the end of his 'winds of change' speech that 'boycotts will never get you anywhere'." (Hyam and Henshaw 2007, 346) Macmillan favored readmission in 1961, it was a sign of the closeness of the relationship that one of Vorwoerd's concerns in withdrawing the application for admission was the impact it would have on Britain. "I could not place them in the invidious position of having to choose between South Africa and a group of Afro-Asian states." (Barber and Hill 1983, 10)

Part of the concern from the 1950s forward was the bipolar world configuration arising. "Perceived Cold War needs were similarly shaping British policy far beyond the Atlantic, Europe and the Middle East. Despite the moves of a new South African government toward apartheid, the Labour cabinet continued to cultivate close political and defence ties for the security of imperial interests in Africa and the alternative route to the Far East." (Bartlett, 1989, 86) The question of sanctions arose periodically, but "successive governments refused to be drawn over the issue of sanctions to South Africa." (Filby 2015, 291) An exchange in the House of Commons in 1986 would seem to confirm this: "The Government do not belive in general economic sanctions; the Labour Government did not believe in general economic sanctions when they were in power, the European Community does not believe in general economic sanctions, the leader of the SDP does not believe in general economic sanctions, the deputy leader of the Labour Party does not believe in general economic sanctions." (Hansard 1 July 1986)

The issue of apartheid and various aspects of the relationship with South Africa were revisited several times. "Following the Sharpeville massacre in 1960, the British recognized apartheid as a matter of international concern and openly started to voice their criticism." (Barber and Hill 1983, 14) In 1973, a government report recommended the constructive engagement approach, but by 1979, a BCC report recommended the approach be abandoned for having failed. (Barber and Hill 1983, 77)

Thatcher was realistic about Britain's standing in absolute terms. "As a famous, if atypical, line in her autobiography expresses it, Britain '…was a middle-ranking power, given unusual influence by virtue of its historical distinction, skilled diplomacy, and versatile military forces – but greatly weakened by economic decline.' None of her predecessors would have thought of Britain in these terms, let alone spoken of it thus." (Sharp 2003, 261) There was only so much that could be done. In nearby Rhodesia as well as other conflicts in southern Africa, Britain was limited in its response in part due to the expense, diplomatically and economically, major action would require. However, because of Britain's ongoing contacts and refusal to enforce major sanctions, "Instead of being the mentor and accepted leader, Britain was often treated as the repentant sinner; the imperialist who had (rather late, perhaps) realized the error of former ways." (Tinker 1977, 78)

In some areas, however, symbolic sanctions seemed to have an impact, perhaps disproportionate to any economic or political reality. "One of the most significant boycotts was in sport. In a post-colonial age, segregated sport became a major international issue. Demonstrations began in 1960 in New Zealand. Verwoerd and Vorster invited reprisals when they refused permission for Maori members to tour with an All Blacks rugby team in 1965 and for ex-Capetonian coloured cricketer Basil D'Oliveira to join the English touring party in 1968." (Beinart 2001, 230) The sporting boycott became formalized in the Gleneagles Agreement in 1977, supported by the Commonwealth, and spilling over into other venues, such as the Olympics. This "convinced anti-apartheid activists that sport was one way of bringing international shame on the Pretorian government." (Filby 2015, 290) These kinds of sanctions are different from general economic sanctions, however. Even in the Falklands crisis, Thatcher mistrusted the effectiveness of general economic sanctions: "Such sanctions are slow to operate and tend to not be wholly successful as there is a good deal of leakage through third countries." (Hansard 26 April 1982)

It was the reality of apartheid, however, and the experience of it that began to make an impact. Geoffrey Howe, future Foreign Secretary under Margaret Thatcher, made a trip to Soweto (that he describes as somewhat clandestine, and certainly unauthorized) in 1975. "The real tensions of apartheid were conveyed to me in those few minutes: the fears and hatreds of a system in which the upholders of the law were almost entirely drawn from a community other than the one they sought to police; and in which, even in our company, our guide was obliged to behave almost as an alien in her own country." (Howe, 1995, 477)

The press, television, movies and more were making the apartheid less theoretical. Some began to equate the situation with the Nazi regime: Jack Ashley in the House of Commons asked, "Is the right hon. Lady failing or refusing to see the obvious parallels between the South African regime today and the regime in Germany in the mid-1930s, with its belief in no democracy, no free speech, a super-race, inferior citizens, and police repression?" (Hansard 1 July 1986) But as a moral issue, it was just one of many, and a subordinate one at that, to Margaret Thatcher, who at this time was about to become Prime Minister for what would effectively amount to the remainder of the era of apartheid.

7 RHODESIA

Rhodesia, "as Margaret Thatcher put it, had become 'a long-standing cause of grief to successive British governments'. Even US Secretary of State Henry Kissinger had tried and failed to defuse this time bomb." (Renwick 2015, 8) The problems of Rhodesia were similar to those of South Africa in terms of racial issues, but different in many other respects. Nonetheless, it had proven difficult to manage. Upon Thatcher's assumption of the office of Prime Minister, to her surprise, the Foreign Office suggested a bolder and "purely British initiative" that had the virtue also of dovetailing with the overall desires of the Commonwealth leaders, in essence, that a white oppressive government not be supported and allowed to remain. (Renwick 2015, 12) In her memoirs, Thatcher wrote, with regard to Rhodesia, "Britain had demonstrated her ability, by a combination of honest dealing and forceful diplomacy, to settle one of the most intractable disputes arising from her colonial past." (Thatcher 1993, 78)

The situation had changed. "When the Portuguese empire in Africa collapsed overnight," O'Sullivan (2016) states, it changed the geopolitics significantly, and that Rhodesia and South Africa became much more fragile. Rhodesia, given its position as a landlocked nation with less development and resources, was under greater stress. Thatcher's initial reaction was against sanctions, interference and pressure, but with help of advisors, she modified her position. "In 1979 at Lusaka Mrs Thatcher had delighted her Commonwealth colleagues by changing her mind on Rhodesia. In 1985 at Nassau she infuriated them by refusing to change her mind on South Africa." (Barber 1988, 110) While unhappy overall with Robert Mugabe, Thatcher did take credit for the successful transition in Rhodesia, noting that sanctions over time had not worked, and that that would be a road down which she was unwilling to trod again. (Moore 2016, 556) Cradock (1997) cites Rhodesia as a striking early success for Thatcher; Barber (1983) states that it served to highlight the central importance of South Africa in the subcontinent. Thatcher would cite Rhodesia in the future defense of her actions with regard to South Africa. "Sanctions have never been known to bring about internal change. Sanctions in Rhodesia did not bring about internal change. The matter had to be resolved by negotiation." (Hansard 1 July 1986)

8 THATCHER'S PHILOSOPHIES AND POLICIES

When Margaret Thatcher succeeded as Prime Minister, there were a few major issues that were center stage – the economy and the Cold War. "Thatcherism was associated, or indeed identified, not only with the concern for economics but with a particular view of economics." (Letwin 1992, 115) In her speeches, Thatcher was always the free market champion: "That means action to free markets, action to widen choice, action to reduce government intervention. Our aim should not be more and more detailed regulation from the centre; it should be to deregulate and to remove the constraints on trade. Britain has been in the lead to opening its markets to others." (Thatcher 1988)

She espoused free trade and fewer restrictions in theory, but this didn't always play out in practice: "Thatcherism has been such a contradictory phenomenon in government."[2] (Gamble, 1988, 232) Wapshott (2007) argues that social issues were very much on the back burner for her. (89) During much of her tenure, the opposition parties were ineffective. ""Opposition disarray enhanced Margaret Thatcher's authority and she knew how to use it." (Biffen 2013, 421) It was also the case that those committed to Thatcher and Thatcherism were something outside politics as usual. "The Thatcher Government is still unusual for the way in which its Leader and some of its principal figures remained committed to a distinctive ideology, and for the extent to which it did attempt in some areas to formulate and carry through a strategy." (Gamble 1988, 222)

But the support of capitalism was never in doubt.   "Under   Margaret   Thatcher   the

---

[2] See here also Simon Jenkins' book, *Thatcher and Sons*, in which he argues that the drive toward centralized control in increasing areas over the terms of Thatcher and her successors in fact was the exact opposite of her stated philosophy of government.

Conservatives have abandoned the hegemonic projects of the past. … The advocacy of the free market is not in conflict with the state being strong. On the contrary, it has been the attempt to restore the free market which has highlighted once more the authority of the state." (Gamble 1988, 172) A stronger economy, in her view, would lead to stronger influence in Europe, in the Commonwealth, and beyond. Her philosophy extended to other nations, too, including South Africa. "Thatcher accepted the argument that politically illiberal states with liberal economies would, sooner rather than later, be forced to reform by the requirements of intellectual-moral consistency and their own economic success." (Sharp 1997, 228) She saw this already happening in South Africa, as the black population became more skilled and educated. "The opponents of apartheid never seemed to her to grasp that capitalism itself was a force for reform and political change, eroding the apartheid laws and creating a black middle class which ultimately would insist on a share of power." (Renwick 2013, 185) She also believed that continuing relations with South Africa bring a better result. "She believed that British influence could do more for the multi-racial future of South Africa by engaging with it than by shunning it." (Moore 2016, 544)

Thatcher had other concerns in this direction, too. There were "cultural and personal ties, and economic links which merge into strategic concerns about the supply of 'vital' minerals and the defence of the Cape route." (Barber and Hill 1983, 3) As Barber and other commentators point out, there was the concern that a black pro-communist government could ally itself with the Soviet Union, and cause a geopolitical shift of power in the region. "She tended to view the problems in South Africa through two prisms: her ideological war with communism and her opposition to terrorism." (Filby 2015, 293)

Moore (2016) sees all these things fitting together: "Three factors predominated in her mind – the importance of British trade and kinship with South Africa, a desire to bring a peaceful end to apartheid and white minority rule, and a Cold War fear of Soviet adventurism in the region." (545) In her autobiography, Thatcher also makes clear her multi-faceted concerns. "Even if it had been morally acceptable to pursue a policy which would have led to the collapse of South Africa, it would not therefore have made strategic sense." (Thatcher 1993, 513) In the Commons, Thatcher was clear about this former equation, that sanctions would likely cause "fundamental strategic problems, putting the supply of raw materials into the hands of the Soviet Union and causing strategic defence problems. It would not bring about the change which we all wish to see." (Hansard 1 July 1986)

Filby (2015) states that while Margaret Thatcher was always vulnerable to the charge that she put British jobs and the economy before the injustices of apartheid, that in fact it was a more consistent point with her; she opposed sanctions against the Soviet Union and other nations, also. (292-4) "She expressed doubts about sanctions. She said that they were hypocritical, because they were not applied to regimes that repressed their people on the basis of something other than race, and cruel, because they caused unemployment and suffering amongst the black population." (Vinen 2009, 222) Riddle (1991) writes that it had long been the British government's view, continued by

Thatcher, that increasing sanctions against South Africa would have the effect of making them more intransigent and repressive of their black population, as well as of their neighbors. (197) It was also the case that Thatcher and her closest advisors didn't see sanctions as effective in bringing about results. "Sanctions were a favourite means of expressing international indignation and they no doubt left a sense of achievement and well-being in the minds of those who voted for them. … But the examples of oppressive governments brought down or obnoxious policies reversed as a result of their application were rare indeed." (Cradock,1997, 146) As Renwick (2015) points out, there were already many forms of sanctions being applied (military, nuclear, oil, sports) but that more sanctions would increase the "siege mentality of the Afrikaners as well as destroy the livelihoods of large numbers of black South Africans." (24)

One final thing argues against the idea that Thatcher was pro-apartheid or even disproportionately pro-South African. "One clear fact is that Thatcher rarely gave a member of the pro-South Africa and Rhodesia lobby any office that might have given them influence over government policy." (Vinen 2009, 222) However, she did keep more control over the process than most, and perhaps any, of her predecessors, due to her antipathy toward the formal structures in place for foreign policy advice and implementation.

9 THATCHER AND SANCTIONS

Support for sanctions had the consensus of the Commonwealth through almost all of Thatcher's term of office, and most of the rest of the world by the end of her term. But Thatcher was not a consensus politician. "Thatcher's style was deliberately confrontational. She made no secret of the fact that she intended to blow apart misbegotten notions of consensus." (Evans 2013, 47) She held this not just as a political belief, but as a religious and philosophical ideal as well. She said, "The Old Testament prophets did not say, 'Brothers I want a consensus.' They said: 'This is my faith, this is what I passionately believe. If you believe it, too, then come with me." (Jeffries 2013) And one of her deep-seated beliefs was that sanctions did not work.

In the first place, this was in keeping with previous British governments of both parties, and consistently within her party. "Evidence seems to point to broad continuity between Conservative policy after 1979 and that of earlier administrations." (Buller 1996, 240) One of the principle reasons for this is that sanctions would seem to be detrimental to businesses at home. When the Commonwealth suggested sanctions and other actions against South Africa early in her tenure, she went along with most suggestions apart from sanctions. "Mrs Thatcher is prepared to go along with most parts of the package, but not with the sanctions. She is opposed to economic sanctions in any form, and even to the threat of sanctions, because she believes that they would not work and would damage Britain's extensive economic interests." (Ashford 1985)

Even if Thatcher has been willing to accept the sacrifice of business and jobs for the sake of ending apartheid, she was not convinced of the likely success of such action. It would be done for nothing, in her view. As she said in the Commons, "There could be no way in which economic sanctions would work in South Africa, with its enormous coastline and with considerable numbers of countries and people who would bend all their efforts to conducting trade with South Africa which other countries would forgo. We should be embarking upon the whole thing for nothing. We should have more unemployment here, only to see the jobs picked up elsewhere. It would damage the cause of black South Africans, the economy of South Africa and the prospect of a peaceful South Africa finally emerging." (Hansard, Statement, 1 July 1986) The effectiveness of participation in sanctions was also in question – Thatcher did not believe a series of comprehensive sanctions would be in fact be honored. "Trade sanctions could be effective only if strictly observed by each and every nation. No universal agreement to impose them has ever been reached." (Hansard, Written Answers, 16 April 1986)

The harming of the innocents, in this case, the oppressed black population, was also a concern of hers. Even though it is usually not a stated policy, for sanctions to succeed it often requires an increase in the suffering of those it is trying to help. "When governments impose sanctions on people in another country, the main goal of the officials who favor the policy is to harm the person or people in charge of that country's government so that they will change their policies. That's the goal. What they do to achieve it is *intentionally* harm many innocent people in those countries, in this case by trying to reduce their supply of gasoline. The sanctions often work in a limited sense: they impose some harm on innocent people in the target country." (Henderson 2009) This seemed to be the case in South Africa. Already the white government was becoming more difficult over time. "The impact of economic sanctions is more likely to harm people, especially the poorest, while authoritarian regimes become more repressive." (Preeg 1995) Thatcher made this clear in her statement to the Commons in 1989: "Our view on apartheid is clear and our practical help for South Africa is clear, as is our hatred of economic sanctions. The hon. Gentleman is one of those who wish to impose punitive economic sanctions—[Interruption.] Economic sanctions are punitive.

That is the only way in which they can work. If the hon. Gentleman is not in favour of that, he must be very glad that our way prevailed and that black South Africa will not suffer from punitive economic sanctions." (Hansard, CHOGM, 26 October 1989)

Ultimately, Thatcher's argument against sanctions was not complicated. "The case against sanctions was simply made. Their likelihood of bringing about a positive change in the policy of the South African government was doubtful at best." (Sharp 1997, 229) As Thatcher said in response during a Prime Minister's Question Time: "I know of no country where sanctions have been effective as an instrument to bring about internal change. That is the point in this case. Sanctions have never been known to bring about internal changes." (Hansard, Question Time, 1 July 1986) The known negatives outweighed the unknown potential positives. "Within Britain, the government's emphasis on the possible economic costs of sanctions was generally successful in preventing the demands for tougher measures gaining support." (Sharp 1997, 230) It also created a complication to other negotiations. "Sanctions were seen as a judgement and as a supplement to the increasing internal pressures on the apartheid system which, from the point of view of the western great powers, often complicated a patient diplomacy they had been conducting." (Sharp 1997, 226)

It is still the case that sanctions are controversial as a tactic. "Economic sanctions are common, albeit controversial, tools of foreign policy. They entail restricting the target states' access to markets in particular goods or services to coerce them into altering their behavior."(Gaskarth 2013, 150) In the text *Economic Sanctions Reconsidered*, first published in 1985, and now in a third edition dated 2009, 200 cases of sanctions in the twentieth century were considered. Only thirteen come in as having been considered successful. "This is not the most reassuring batting average. And it appears that many of the best-known sanctions, such as those against South Africa during apartheid, were probably not home runs." (Taylor 2014) Thatcher's belief that sanctions were more for window dressing also seems to continue to be borne out in many cases. "In a world bristling with bad actors, and especially at a time when the country is wary of another war, sanctions have an obvious appeal—and limited impact. Sanctions have failed to dissuade Iran from continuing to enrich uranium. They haven't dislodged North Korea's repressive and erratic leaders or forced a rollback of their nuclear and missile programs. For all the international pressure on Syria's Assad, the regime is getting more ruthless, not less, and the policy debate in Washington has moved on to how much military support to provide the rebels." (Robbins 2013) But sanctions sometimes do have an effect – according to Doxey, "sanctions are more effective against democratic regimes than authoritarian regimes." (1996) Perhaps it is true that most cases of sanctions fail because most cases are not against democratic nations.

10 THATCHER AND THE FOREIGN OFFICE

Thatcher's mistrust of the Foreign Office grew during her time in office, but she came in with suspicions already.[3] Gaskarth (2013), in his recent text on British foreign policy, states, "Prime

---

[3] Barber and Hill (1983) recounts a pattern that illustrated the concerns: "There have even been differences within the Foreign Office. The memory is still clear of Lord Caradon's visits to Whitehall during his period as British representative to the United Nations. He would return full of enthusiasm from New York to urge greater efforts against South Africa and Rhodesia only to find that his sense of urgency was not always matched in London and even less in the British embassy in Pretoria. Between the departments there is constant bargaining and jockeying for position so that the 'official view' is usually a compromise of departmental positions." (88)

ministerial dominance of the foreign policy agenda has been highly controversial, leading some to see the office as becoming more 'presidential'. A number of commentators trace this belief to Margaret Thatcher's period in office." (14) While there were many factors in determining the success or workability of a policy, "It was the FCO that would be singled out as an obstacle to the prime minister's policy agenda."(Gaskarth 2013, 14) Moore's official biography of Thatcher explains this as in part due to a difference of philosophy and focus. "South African sanctions provides a classic example of Mrs Thatcher in action – reaching over policy elites and foreign leaders by reiterating what she saw as home truths, putting up with isolation in the belief that she would be proved right later."(Moore 2016, 569) South Africa was not the only example of this, however. In her autobiography, she wrote, "I not more shared the established Foreign Office view of Africa than I did of the Middle East."[4] (Thatcher 1993, 512)

---

[4] It is perhaps ironic that, according to Buller (1996), she often seemed concerned to continue the pre-1979 foreign policy directions that charting new courses. (230)

In particular, Thatcher saw the Foreign Office as the champion of sanctions that she did not support. "While, on occasions, the FCO as favoured 'symbolic' sanctions to avoid alienating other Western and Commonwealth countries, Mrs Thatcher has stood firmly against them." (Barber 1988, 100) As a result, she began increasingly relying on personal and party advisors rather than the Foreign Office.[5] It didn't matter to her that she ran the risk of standing alone. "Thatcher's response was to assume a tighter grip on South African policy by cutting the Foreign Office from her deliberations, the better to maintain her line of no substantive concessions to the pressure for sanctions. The threat of diplomatic isolation was, for her at least, an empty one."(Sharp 1997, 234) The tension on this issue was complex, but often cast in simplistic, racial lines. "Margaret Thatcher in her memoirs unfairly claims that the Foreign

---

[5] From the start, there seemed to be a conflict in the making by her decisions on how to staff the offices responsible. "The team chosen for the Foreign Office and Defence in 1979 – Carrington, Gilmour and Pym – were clearly not members of the Thatcherite clan. Hence the future of Conservative foreign policy after May 1979 was obscure." (Bulpitt 1988, 190)

Office wanted to sell out South to black Africa."(Cradock 1997, 149)   Also, "The *New Statesman's* blunt assessment was that: 'For Mrs Thatcher, South Africa is a "white" country and she gives every sign of hoping that events will keep it that way."(Hyam and Henshaw 2007, 336)

She even excluded frequently her own Foreign Secretary, Geoffrey Howe, who also had the distinction of being perhaps her longest serving and most loyal Cabinet minister. "South Africa became one of those subjects for which Mrs Thatcher and Powell worked out the direction of policy at the highest level and cut out Geoffrey Howe and his officials."(Moore 2016, 568) Despite his public loyalty and statements of support in the House (Barber 1988, 105), it was becoming a point of contention between them. In his memoirs, Howe (1995) wrote, "South Africa could be counted on to provoke instinctively different reactions from Margaret Thatcher and myself. The tension was often obvious. Yet our taut partnership did, I think, play its part in prompting positive change." (476) Near the end of her premiership, as South African President F.W. de Klerk was preparing to make significant changes, her disdain for the Foreign Office remained high. "I told the Foreign Office – who did not like it one bit – that as soon as Mr Mandela was freed I wanted us to respond rapidly by rescinding or relaxing the measures we had taken against South Africa." (Thatcher 1993, 531) Despite foreign policy successes during her term, Howe saw her attitude as unfortunate, at best. "The sadness is that Margaret Thatcher, right to the end, persisted in her often ill-conceived antipathy toward most of our Commonwealth partners as also toward the Foreign and Commonwealth Office and all its works – as though it had nothing to do with the devoted and detailed work that so many people put in on her behalf." (Howe 1995, 500)

11 DOMESTIC POLITICS

There is a saying that there are no votes in foreign policy. While Barber could report in 1983 that "South Africa has become ingrained in the British domestic political debate in a way which is unusual for foreign affairs," (46), he would later write, "South Africa has not been an issue in any of Mrs Thatcher's three elections as a Conservative party leader." (Barber 1988, 102) Cradock (1997) reported that "the quarrels with the Commonwealth over South Africa excited much media comment but probably had little impact on the general public." (31) This illustrated "a paradox between electoral neglect and vigourous activities at other times."(Barber and Hill 1983, 51) Even at the critical point after the collapse of the Eminent

Persons Group mission and increased pressure from the Commonwealth, public opinion seemed divided but somewhat supportive of Thatcher's actions: "Since 1 May 1986 I have receive about 2,800 letters opposing, and about 5,900 supporting the Government's stand on sanctions against South Africa. No further breakdown of these figures is available." (Hansard, Written Answers, 12 January 1987)

Part of the issue was the fact that while most in Britain condemned apartheid, they also condemned violence and hoped for peaceful reform. (Barber and Hill 1983, 6) The Conservatives were more inclined than others to let the situation sort itself out, but governments under Labour had also been disinclined to take more decisive action, and none seriously contemplated dramatic intervention. However, as Thatcher's tenure continued, there were some shifts. "British attitudes toward South Africa were, nevertheless, more polarized than ever in the 1980s, as Thatcher, her government, and her supporters strongly resisted aggressive action against Pretoria. The resistance, in turn, increased the tendency to condemn apartheid as a means of opposing Thatcherism more generally."(Hyam and Henshaw 2007, 331)

The business community from the 1960s forward tried to keep a low profile in the media while working to influence the continuing of trade and business connections. Malcolm Rifkind, a minister at the Foreign Office, stated that the business community, even among the whites of South Africa, saw "that apartheid is a system without a future. ...it is indeed the business community of South Africa that has been in the forefront of the process of reform." (Barber 1988, 104) This was cited by the business community as reason to keep trade and business going. The UK/South Africa Trade Association (UKSATA), while typically working outside mainstream media attention, nevertheless worked to impress the importance of the business community and the damage that could be done with widespread sanctions. UKSAT estimated as many as 250,000 jobs could be lost in Britain alone; these figures were disputed by others who saw the statistics as inflated. But Thatcher used large yet vague statistics in her speeches: at the 1986 Conservative

Party conference, she said (contrasting her party with Labour), "Labour wants sanctions against South Africa. Tens of thousands of people could lose their jobs in Britain – quite apart from the devastating consequences for black South Africans." (Harris 1997, 260)

It was the case, however, that at the start of Thatcher's time in office, "roughly 10 per cent of all British overseas investments are in South Africa, but the rate of return has often been about 16 per cent of the total."(Barber and Hill 1983, 32) This would seem like a good rate of return. However, there was an ethical issue that the British business world tended to ignore. "They travel the world telling people what fantastic profits can be made by investing in South Africa. Of course they say they are opposed to apartheid, but they shy away from the point that these super-profits are only possible because apartheid generates a virtually limitless supply of cheap black labour." (Harrison 1985, 168) Both British business associations and the Government recognized one more fact about the modern world, the increasing lack of control by any given government. "The

Government's ability to control international economic transactions is declining, as relationships grow more complex, and as more and more business and financial institutions are organized along multinational lines." (Barber and Hill 1983, 30)

Another key constituency on the opposite side was the Anti-Apartheid Movement (AAM). This, according to Filby (2015), was "incredibly well organized…; an umbrella organization of church groups, left-win activists, trade union supporters, local councils and a strong following of Liberal and Labour politicians." (290) The British Council of Churches (BCC) was a key player in this as well. As early as 1965 they identified the issue of apartheid as a moral one in theological terms: their report of that year "stated clearly that apartheid is a blasphemy against the Holy Spirit and it raised the spectre of race war, but the group showed no sympathy either for the use of force or even sanctions against South Africa."(Barber and Hill 1983, 75)

Anglican church leaders had been involved in action as early as the 1940s: Michael Scott, John

Collins, and particularly Trevor Huddleston would lead the cause, with increasing support from the church hierarchy but consistent support from the left.[6] "For some Conservatives, though, the Church's uncompromising stance on South Africa was yet further evidence of its tendency to wrap left-wing causes in a Christian guise."(Filby 2015, 295). This is perhaps ironic, given that Margaret Thatcher joined the Anglican church after her marriage to Denis Thatcher, giving up her Methodism for "the more socially respectable creed of Anglicanism and membership of the state-aligned Church of England, whose importance in defining and maintaining the English hierarchy had long led it to be dubbed 'the Conservative Party at prayer'." (Wapshott 2007, 31)

At a time when the South Africa officialdom as still trying to portray Nelson Mandela and other

---

[6] Trevor Huddleston would become in many ways the public face of the anti-apartheid movement in Britain. When Thatcher gave an interview after meeting with PW Botha in 1984, repeating her demands to him to begin the dismantling of apartheid and the release of Nelson Mandela, Huddleston sent a handwritten note of thanks to her. Later Mandela would say of Huddleston, "No white person has done more for South Africa." (Renwick 2015, 26, and Filby 2015, 289).

anti-apartheid leaders as socialists, communists, and terrorists, it was from the church that another anti-apartheid leader emerged. 'Christian leaders in South Africa became the leading voices of resistance to state ideology and in Desmond Tutu the opposition movement had a legitimate spokesperson who could not simply be dismissed as a terrorist or a communist; indeed, Tutu always described communism as being as evil as apartheid and condemned violence as much as state oppression." (Filby 2015, 291) It was the increase in violence and oppression that also leant substance to the moral claims that could be accepted beyond the church walls. "It was also obvious to anyone who followed the extensive British news coverage of South Africa that the maintenance of white power through the most violent and brutal suppression of apartheid's opponents was morally unjustifiable." (Hyam and Henshaw 2007, 337)

12 THATCHER AND P.W. BOTHA

P.W. Botha became Prime Minister of South Africa a few years prior to Margaret Thatcher's election. In 1981, Edward Heath, former Prime Minister of Britain, had visited and made a speech in which he claimed that reforms before then had been inadequate, and said, "unless and until the dismantlement of apartheid is assured, it would be a grave mistake for South Africa to base her strategy on the assumption that when the chips are down the West will stand with her." (Barber and Hill 1983, 53) Botha supported a new constitution; his constitutional position changed in 1984 when he became state president with sweeping powers. "Within South Africa, President P.W. Botha had started by presenting himself as a modernizing reformer, though none of his changes gave any effective representation to the black community."(Renwick 2013, 184) The changes enacted included legislative chambers for "coloured" and "Indians" but not for blacks, who were still excluded, and at least initially expected to emigrate to homelands that would become separate, but subordinate, nations. However, with everything still subject to executive control, not much effectively changed in terms of race relations overall. Despite the appeals from leaders, including Thatcher, to work toward abolishing apartheid, "Botha's objective was to modernize apartheid, not to get rid of it." (Renwick 2015, 26)

Despite these set-backs, Thatcher was still determined to employ constructive engagement rather than increased sanctions and pressure. This included a controversial visit by P.W. Botha to Britain to meet with her. "The deep division in British attitudes toward South Africa was especially evident in the response to P.W. Botha's controversial visit to London and Chequers in 1984. His purpose was to meet Britain's prime minister, the staunch Cold Warrior and dogmatic free-marketer, Margaret Thatcher."(Hyam and Henshaw 2007, 333) Thatcher was criticized for extending the invitation, but responded that she would not shy away from making contact with governments with whom Britain was at odds, and used the Soviet Union as a prime example. (Barber 1988, 99)

Part of Thatcher's idea might have been to engage him personally, not just professionally. According to Moore (2016), she found him extremely prickly with an instinctive anti-Britishness. (547) Renwick (2013) describes him as being found "charmless and inflexible," but that it was still important to go forward with the attempt. "Thatcher's aim was to bring Botha back in from the diplomatic cold and to coax him into reforms, which holding off the international pressure. This was a legitimate strategy as long as Botha was willing to comply, but he was not." (Filby 2015, 294) According to Geoffrey Howe (1995), his response to the calls for ending apartheid and releasing Nelson Mandela met with the response, "You won't force South Africans to commit national suicide." (491)

On her part, Thatcher tried repeatedly to get some movement on the issues with P.W. Botha. After the Commonwealth agreed to a mission (the Eminent Persons Group, or EPG; see more below), "Mrs Thatcher wrote to Botha, maintaining her support for the EPG concept very clearly: 'a commitment to the early release of Nelson Mandela and the unbanning of the ANC, in exchange for a suspension of violence, would do more than any other step to create the climate of confidence in which a dialogue would become possible." (Moore 2016, 568-9) On his part, Botha would try to shift the focus toward other issues he thought would resonate with Thatcher. He tried to use events such as the invasion of Afghanistan and the production of "secret documents" about a communist party plot to take over the government, but it didn't seem to have much effect.[7] His use of the military and police forces, in particular declaring states of emergency giving his already broad powers greater

---

[7] Thatcher's close advisor, Charles Powell, on reading about the letters about a communist plot, dismissed their importance, and "commented drily: 'That's what Communist parties are like'." (Moore 2016, 567)

ferocity, made him untrustworthy as a reformer.

Renwick (2013) tries to soften the image of P.W. Botha with now declassified material detailing some covert contacts with the ANC and Mandela, and shifts some of the blame for the maintenance of apartheid onto the military and "securocrats" in charge.[8] However, Botha's post presidential career saw him continue to fight against the changes that were by then clearly taking place in a more peaceful, democratic manner. Near the end of his time as president, special advisor Fritz Leutwiler (a Swiss banker by profession), "reported subsequently to the Prime Minister that the last-ditch atmosphere around P.W. Botha was like that which must have prevailed around Hitler in his bunker."(Renwick 2015, 69)

It is perhaps ironic that one of the key issues internal to the Afrikaner population was the arms sanctions, according to Papenfus (2011): "When Mrs Thatcher was returned to power for a second term in 1983 the news was rather coolly received

---

[8] Renwick (2013) at the same time can be scathing; he described P.W. Botha thus: "His domed head and tinted glasses gave him the appearance of a B-movie villain." (189)

by the pro-government Afrikaans-language press."[9] (340-1) Pik Botha (foreign minister, not to be confused with P.W. Botha) said that it was Thatcher who was the racist, as "she wanted South Africa to be judged in Western terms and not by African standards." (Papenfus 2011, 341) Pik Botha was seen as a liberal (within the context of National Party politics); he stated publically that he could see South Africa with a black president – a speech he was made to disavow as a personal statement and not at all reflective of the government. However, he also staunchly defended his nation's interests; when Howe met with him and mentioned sanctions, Pik Botha's response was sharp: "If sanctions are applied, we shall make damn sure our neighbours suffer, and suffer a damn sight more than we do!"(Howe 1995, 490)

Ultimately, Thatcher was looking for a reformer. "She had perhaps overestimated her own

---

[9] And Thatcher, while accepting the arms sanctions, still pointed out the difficulty generally with sanctions. "We have rigourously enforced mandatory sanctions on arms to South Africa. Nevertheless, South Africa does not seem to be short of certain things." (Hansard, Question Time, 19 June 1986)

powers of persuasion. Botha was no Gorbachev and certainly not the man to enact change in South Africa."(Filby 2015, 295) In her autobiography, Thatcher (1993) wrote, "I had always felt that fundamental reform would never take place while P.W. Botha was president." (529) Even so, increased sanctions were not on the table. Helen Suzman, progressive politician and South African anti-apartheid advocate, said "she [Thatcher] was right to oppose comprehensive sanctions and to work for peaceful change, but she must not expect anything positive from P.W. Botha. We had to work on those likely to succeed him."[10](Renwick 2013, 201)

---

[10] Helen Suzman was even mentioned by name in a give-and-take during Prime Minister's Question Time. Kinnock was arguing for added pressure via sanctions; Thatcher was once again resistant to the idea, and using Suzman's stature as a South African politician more on the Labour side of the spectrum, who was also against increased sanctions, as a support. (Hansard, Question Time, 17 June 1986)

13 THATCHER AND F.W. DE KLERK

Pik Botha would play a role in helping with the transition. Howe would say of Pik Botha, "Yet through all this prickly defensive talk I thought I detected a man with real insight into the imperative need for his country to change – and to change fundamentally. My judgment has, I think, been confirmed over subsequent years in which we came to know each other well."(Howe 1995, 478-9) During the nadir of P.W. Botha's presidency, Pik Botha met with both Thatcher and Howe, and announced in an upbeat fashion to a journalist, "the season of violence is past." (Papenfus 2011, 593)

F.W. de Klerk was an unlikely reformer, having come up in the same political party and environment as his predecessor. He was not P.W. Botha's choice as successor, but was still considered to be of the same conservative ideology – the ANC denounced him upon his appointment and subsequent election (President Botha had had a stroke while in office, and was ultimately forced to resign both party leadership and the presidency). When as party leader in 1989 he came to visit Thatcher at Chequers, the AAM picketed the visit. However, Thatcher repeated her own anti-apartheid expectations to him. "In fact, Mrs Thatcher made clear to de Klerk, with her customary lack of ambiguity, the need to get on with the Namibia settlement and to release Mandela."(Renwick 2015, 96)

Thatcher saw in de Klerk the leader she had been waiting for, and was determined to help him succeed, although it is unlikely she foresaw how rapidly change would take place. "It was surely right to give the new South African leader the opportunity to make his mark without ham-fisted outside intervention."(Thatcher 1993, 529) In the transition, "the influence we were able to exert derived essentially from Margaret Thatcher. De

Klerk was far more disposed to listen to her than to any other foreign leader, and the ANC, once reassured of our commitment to genuine majority rule, looked to us to help overcome obstacles with the South African government."(Renwick 2013, 209) Thatcher was even invited to South Africa, but the situation, both politically and safety-wise, made it impossible. "There was, I knew, nothing more likely to sour his [de Klerk's] dealings with other governments who had been proved wrong about South Africa than for me to arrive in his country as a kind of proclamation that I had been right."(Thatcher 1993, 532-3) With regard to safety, it was considered unsafe for Thatcher, given that right-wing extremists had fired shots into the British embassy in Pretoria shortly after de Klerk's lifting of the state of emergency and announcing fundamental reforms, including the release of Mandela and the dismantling of apartheid.[11]

------

[11] F.W. de Klerk is himself a complicated figure. Renwick (2013) states that "South Africa thereby became the only country ever to develop a nuclear weapon capability and then renounce it. For this act alone, de Klerk deserved the Nobel Prize." (206) On the other hand, Anthony Sampson (1999) accuses de Klerk of allowing his ministers to set up

Thatcher would have to wait until after her tenure as Prime Minister had concluded before she would be able to visit South Africa.

---

their own criminal empires and of being complicit in ANC violence. (442-4)

14 THATCHER AND THE COMMONWEALTH

Margaret Thatcher was perhaps most contentious, with regard to South Africa, when it came to her dealings with the Commonwealth. She "came to regard the Commonwealth as a pointless hangover from the days of empire, in which Third World dictators would use the institution to hector properly elected leaders of democracies." (Palmer 2015, 105) The Commonwealth had meetings every other year of all heads of government, with the Queen as the nominal head of the organization. With successive meetings, the tone went from bad to worse. It was rarely helpful, in Thatcher's view. She thought it "a tiresome obstacle to realistic foreign policy." (Palmer 2015, 105) As Barber (1983) states, the Commonwealth is oddly named, for the countries did not have common interests much of the time, and as an international organization, it was neither sharp nor flexible. (17)

At her first Commonwealth Head of Government Meeting (CHOGM) in Melbourne, 1981, she had come off the Rhodesian settlement, and found "Britain was less the focus of international criticism by the Commonwealth than on the previous occasion, and the serious pressure for sanctions against South Africa still lay in the future." (Thatcher 1993, 166) Sharp (1997) indicates that Britain was still seen as the indispensible nation: "Without British support, however, a system of mandatory and comprehensive sanctions could not be imposed on South Africa. Accordingly, when Thatcher came to office in 1979, no such system was in place." (226) However, even then she believed "the Commonwealth liked to treat Britain as a target, not a guiding star." (Moore 2016, 555) That feature remained constant, with the intensity changing over time, with Thatcher's resistance increasing in step. "On the South African issue they had come to resemble a seasonal pageant play, with stock characters, set speeches and only limited bearing on reality, namely the situation inside South Africa. In the casting for these dramas Mrs Thatcher was automatically assigned the villain's role, a part she played, or overplayed, with relish." (Cradock 1997, 153) In her memoirs, Thatcher (1993) quipped, after an uncharacteristic positive move, "Then it was back to more irrationality..." (521)

Thatcher's mistrust of the Foreign Office was acute with regard to the Commonwealth. "The basic, if usually unstated, assumption seemed to be that Britain's national interests required that we should ultimately be prepared to go along with the opinions of the radical black African states in the Commonwealth." (Thatcher 1993, 512) But her mistrust of the Commonwealth, both in terms of many of the other leaders and the organization as a whole, needed no priming. She saw it as an expression of group hypocrisy, and many of her advisors could sense "her irritation at being lectured on human rights and sanctions by African

Presidents who never hesitated to lock up their own political opponents or trade with South Africa." (Renwick 2013, 187) According to Moore (2016), she was annoyed that many Commonwealth nations oppressed their own people on different bases, but "liked to forge a too easy unity over South Africa, designed to put Britain in the dock." (553) Also, many Commonwealth countries carried on trade despite sanctions they had agreed upon, while others who advocated sanctions in fact had no trade or business at risk in doing so.

The most contentious of the CHOGM events was in Nassau, in 1985. Around the table of 46 delegations, "we had few effective allies. Botswana, Lesotho, and Swaziland, geographically tied to the South African economy as closely as any hostages, were silent supporters. Harry Lee Kuan Yew of Singapore was, as so often, a brilliantly wild card, who could sometimes be helpful. But in terms of willingness to argue the case in broad principle we were effectively alone."(Howe 1995, 481) Moore (2016) indicates that she was not above using her gender in the heated negotiations; while presenting a tough line against sanctions, she could still provoke a guilty reaction with the right calculation.(562)

Sanctions were high on the agenda at Nassau. There was near unanimity for them, with Britain the only major holdout. After granting minor and largely symbolic concessions after very spirited debates that had spilled out into the press, she managed to set any goodwill gained aside by a patronizing television interview afterwards. As Howe (1995) relates, "With forefinger and thumb only a few millimeters apart and contemptuously presented to the cameras, Margaret proclaimed that she had moved only 'a tiny little bit'." (483) With that physical gesture, "she had at one and the same time humiliated three dozen other heads of government, devalued the policy on which they had just agreed, and demeaned herself."(Howe 1995, 483) According Howe (1995), Moore (2016) and other commentators, this single image of Thatcher sums up for many her regard for the Commonwealth and for the seriousness of the issue of apartheid. "By giving a little ground Mrs Thatcher had gained an agreed position, but she lost whatever goodwill she had salvaged from her

Commonwealth colleagues by a patronizing television interview in which she disparaged the agreement." (Barber 1988, 113)

One key development that did come from the Nassau meeting was the appointment of the Eminent Persons Group, a mission led by Commonwealth leaders (other than heads of government) who would be both fact-finding and recommendation-offering, to assess whether or not Botha's reforms and the general development of South African society warranted increased pressure or not. The report on the mission, overall deemed a failure, was co-authored by Shridath "Sonny" Ramphal, and stated "Our mandate was to foster a process of negotiation across lines of colour, politics and religion, with a view to establishing a non-racial and representative government." (Fraser and Ramphal 1986, 131) Ramphal stated that the realities of apartheid were appalling, and "none of us was prepared for the reality of apartheid." (Fraser and Ramphal 1986, 22) Not only in terms of conditions, but also in terms of law and politics, the structures of apartheid showed no signs of lessening. "Such an array of state powers, many of which are expressly not subject to review by the Courts, coupled with extraordinarily wide definitions of 'communism', 'terrorism', 'treason' and 'sedition', render the country, in the experience of blacks, a police state with a permanent state of emergency – so much so that lawyers with whom we spoke had been surprised that the Government had found it necessary to impose a formal state of emergency in 1985 unless it were to placate the right wing." (Fraser and Ramphal 1986, 53-5)

Some had seen the EPG as a stalling tactic, as indeed Thatcher's response to the failure of the group to secure any change or promise of change. "Thatcher tried to thwart but succeeded only in snubbing her Commonwealth partners when they voted in favour of tougher economic measures. By way of compromise, the Commonwealth dispatched an Eminent Persons Group to South Africa. Simultaneously, and perhaps not coincidentally, South African attacks on Botswana, Zimbabwe and Zambia scotched any usefulness that it might have." (Calvocoressi 2013, 639) Thatcher's response was to send Geoffrey Howe directly; Howe was hesitant. "Geoffrey was extremely reluctant to go and it must be said that his reluctance proved justified since he was insulted by President Kaunda and brushed off by President Botha."(Thatcher 1993, 520) According to Papenfus (2011) and Howe (1995), there was from the start no realistic expectation that this follow-up to the EPG would succeed. An American observer, Crocker (1994) noted that this assignment for Howe "had all the hallmarks of a kamikaze mission." (306) Both for Thatcher and for South Africa, things settled into an ongoing miserable state. "The years 1986-9, following the collapse of the eminent persons' mission, were arid and painful ones for South Africa and, in consequence, for British diplomacy dealing with the international repercussions of the crisis." (Cradock 1997, 152) According to Fraser (2010), his interactions with Thatcher showed that she was as intractable as ever on the idea of further sanctions: "Of the seven countries that had commissions the group (the EPG), six agreed to adopt broad sanctions against South Africa as a moral imperative. The United Kingdom, on the other hand, agreed only to maintain existing bans." (660) As Riddle (1991) highlights, the issue of sanctions continued, with Britain finally giving in a bit more in conjunction with the European Union, and violence and repressive action and legislation increasing in South Africa.

Subsequent CHOGMs didn't have the same heat as Nassau in 1985, but after the Vancouver meeting in 1987, the meeting "closed with another unhelpful aside from Margaret Thatcher to her closing press conference. It was there that she suddenly lashed out at the ANC – which we had for years been trying to get unbanned – as 'a typical terrorist organization', and once again set back the prospect of dialogue between us and their leadership."(Howe 1995, 499) However, Thatcher pointed out during the meeting that most Commonwealth states and black African states had also failed by that point to impose and enforce general sanctions, and she saw this as vindication of her policy. (Riddle 1991, 197) Canadian Prime Minister and host Brian Mulroney tried to take Britain to task, but Thatcher came armed with figures. "In reply to the sanctimonious criticism of our Canadian hosts, I had figures released which showed that Canada's imports from South Africa had risen. It was a useful comment on the Commonwealth heads' sincerity."(Thatcher 1993, 523) In the Commons, Thatcher said, regarding the Commonwealth's stance, that even though the EPG had failed, its principles were still valid: "I agree that getting negotiation, against the background of the suspension of violence, is the acid test of how to get the dismantlement of apartheid…. Therefore, we fully support the negotiating concept which was defined by the Eminent Persons Group, and which I still believe is the right one." (Hansard, CHOGM, 22 October 1987)

By the time of the Kuala Lumpur CHOGM, which would be Thatcher's last, events were moving swiftly in South Africa, and the group paid little attention to that, in her view. "Considering that it paid no regard whatever to the positive developments in South Africa, she proceeded to issue a statement of her own, paying tribute to those changes and suggesting that the Commonwealth should concentrate on encouraging them, rather than on further punishment." (Renwick 2013, 207) John Major, there as Foreign Secretary, and who would end up as Prime Minister a year later, was not permitted to meet the ANC delegation, and Thatcher later "quibbled over Major's attempts to deal tactfully with the issue of South African sanctions." (Wall 2008, 85) As events unfolded in a positive direction in South Africa, Thatcher felt further vindication that her leadership had been correct. "When [Mulroney] said British leadership of the Commonwealth would be 'imperiled' if she did not give ground at the review conference, she retorted that 'one had to draw a distinction between leadership and followership'." (Moore 2016, 572)

15 THATCHER AND THE QUEEN

Attendant to the Commonwealth issue was the issue of the status of the Queen and her relationship to both Thatcher and the Commonwealth. The Queen is head of the Commonwealth, but is also head of state of the United Kingdom, of which Margaret Thatcher was Prime Minister (not to mention individually head of state of some other Commonwealth nations). The Queen took her Commonwealth status seriously, and despite its place outside of the Commonwealth, still had an historical connection and affection for South Africa. "In a speech delivered during the royal tour of South Africa on 21 April 1947 to mark her coming of age, Elizabeth said, 'I declare before you all that my whole life … shall be devoted to your service and the service of our great imperial Commonwealth to which we all belong.' Elizabeth's passion for Africa would eventually be the cause of major conflict with Margaret Thatcher, and push her towards a very public constitutional crisis." (Palmer 2015, 81)

In an open letter to Queen Elizabeth, Archbishop Desmond Tutu called for her support against apartheid. This raised issues on several levels, because the Queen is also head of the church in which Tutu was an archbishop, a hierarchy at least notionally independent of the party political government; it also brought forward that fact that, as a Commonwealth issue, it was not strictly the concern of the government in Westminster, either. Tutu described apartheid as "the most vicious system since Nazism," a charge that would no doubt resonate with a monarch who served in service during the war against the Nazis. (Moore 2016, 570)

In addition to this, "many made it clear to [the Queen] that Britain was forfeiting its unique place in the leadership of the Commonwealth." (Palmer 2015, 169) It was unusual, but nonetheless true that the dual roles of the Queen – as monarch of the UK and as head of the Commonwealth – could come into conflict. (Barber 1988, 112) Andrew Neil, then editor of the major newspaper, *The Sunday Times*, reported, "the Queen, it was said, did not like Britain being a minority of one; Thatcher's refusal to go along with sanctions had particularly infuriated the Commonwealth's black African leaders, to whom the Queen was especially attached." (Neil 1997, 194) Upon assigning an investigative journalist to follow up on leaked information from the Buckingham Palace Press Office (which later turned out to be Michael Shea, press secretary to the Queen), it seemed "the Queen was unhappy with the whole thrust of Thatcherism. It was an unprecedented insight into a ruling monarch's political views." (Neil 1997, 195)

For her part, Thatcher's antipathy for the Commonwealth was made worse by what she saw as not only hypocrisy of action but also hypocrisy of status. "She was intensely irritated by the whole rigmarole of the Commonwealth – its combination of institutionalized anti-Britishness with riding on the coat-tails of British imperial prestige, its self-importance, and the complications caused by the involvement of the Queen." (Moore 2016, 583) The meetings between the Prime Minister of the UK and the Queen are famously private; from the time of Winston Churchill forward, the Queen has refused to give details of the meetings, and works hard to maintain an apolitical stance, both in domestic and international affairs (as well as the domestic affairs of other nations). As Moore (2016) states, there is no known evidence that Thatcher and the Queen had active disagreements on the subject, but it was clear there was a divergence of interests.[12] In the end, the press stories dominated the papers, no mean feat when it

---

[12] Claire Ellicott, taking advantage of the release of papers under the 30-year rule, wrote in the *Daily Mail*, 'There is a wide view too that the Queen is in a rage with Mrs Thatcher over her handling of the sanctions question (not because of the substance of the argument but because of its style: the Queen, it is said, sees the insensitivity as further damaging "her" Commonwealth at a sensitive time),' he wrote. Such was the Queen's anger she considered scrapping her weekly audience with Mrs Thatcher, the Palace source told Mr Ryan. The Queen can use the audience to express her views on government matters." However, even these statements are based on second-hand accounts. (Ellicott 2017)

meant bumping a royal wedding (that of Andrew and Sarah) off the lead, for a time. But eventually, the leak was identified, and while disavowing any wrongdoing (claiming to have been misquoted), Shea resigned quietly shortly thereafter. (Neil 1997)

Perhaps one final note, from *The Economist*, put a positive spin on the negative press and tense relations Thatcher had with both Queen and Commonwealth. They concluded "that Britain could take the threats as a 'reassuring compliment', for although in principle the 49 Commonwealth members are equal, 'in practice only British actions (or failure to act) are held to be capable of jeopardizing the future of the association'." (*Economist,* 1985)

16 THATCHER AND REAGAN

When Ronald Reagan became president, Margaret Thatcher made it a deliberate point to be the first foreign leader who visited him. According to Wapshott (2007), "at that first meeting, the rapport between the pair was instantaneous and heartfelt." (90) This was a relationship that was political and personal that lasted Reagan's entire tenure in office. "From the first, Reagan and Thatcher decided that they had found a fellow soldier in arms against a common foe, an ally who would undoubtedly prove to be a reliable and loyal friend." (Wapshott 2007, 91) Reagan had shifted foreign policy focus away from the human-rights centered direction of President Carter, which meant in practical terms sometimes "ignoring the human rights of those oppressed by such U.S. allies as General Pinochet, South Africa, or the shah of Iran." (O'Sullivan, 2016, 45) This fit well with Thatcher, who shared Reagan's primary focus on Cold War politics and economic affairs. "While they shared views on economic conservatism and on anti-Communist foreign policy, conservative social issues were ignored. Their future relationship was to continue to hinge solely upon a shared view of economic and foreign matters." (Wapshott 2016, 89) With regard to South Africa, the Reagan administration favored "constructive engagement" just as Thatcher had. (Byrd 1988, 24)

How much impact Reagan and the United States might have had on South Africa was a matter of differing opinion. According to Barber, "While the USA, for instance, has a much greater potential than Britain for exerting influence in South Africa, the issue is seldom a matter of American public concern or inter-party conflict."(Barber and Hill 1983, 8) On the other hand, Crocker (1994) states, "The United States was trying to conduct regional diplomacy with a distinctly weak hand. The region was distant from American experience, a place where we had relatively few tangible assets and no basis for deploying or projecting American power." (39) Perhaps the memory of Kissinger's failure in Rhodesia was in mind here. But Reagan was inclined to follow Thatcher's lead much of the time, and Thatcher returned the loyalty consistently. "Publically, Thatcher – and only Thatcher, among the leaders of the world – supported Reagan unwaveringly, despite massive domestic and international pressure to do otherwise." (Berlinski 2008, 273) Thatcher was aware of the issue of being seen to be weak, or negotiating from a position of weakness – responding to David Owen, former Foreign Secretary, then leader of the Social Democratic Party in Britain, she said, "I do not believe that we are negotiating from weakness in any way." (Hansard, 1 July 1986)

Much like the internal politics of Britain, the domestic politics of United States saw the issue of South Africa as one with importance and various intensity, but little electoral impact or policy traction until the latter half of the 1980s. "There is no deep-rooted American experience of southern Africa on which a consistent response has been built."(Barber and Hill 1983, 22) This made it easier for Reagan to dismiss anti-apartheid activists in the United States as left-wing and outside the mainstream. However, as the decade progressed, and more awareness of the realities of apartheid came to the public consciousness, members of Congress took note, and some of Reagan's subordinates began to shift in their thinking – Geoffrey Howe reported that by the mid-point of Reagan's second (and final) term, Secretary of State George Shultz, with regard to need for increased sanctions, was "already well ahead of Margaret Thatcher on this point." (492)

By 1986, Reagan's authority was diminishing as a lame duck president, with some scandals beginning to mount. In the late summer, there was sufficient support in Congress not only to pass an Anti-Apartheid Act requiring a broad range of sanctions, but enough support for Congress to override the Reagan's veto. The Senate override of Reagan's veto of 1986 Anti-Apartheid Act, despite a televised appeal against it and a very public veto, was "the first time in the twentieth century that it had overturned a presidential veto on foreign policy." (Filby 2015, 295) According to Crocker (1994), Congress took a lead from the Eminent Persons Group: "A series of specific 'conditions' were identified – most of them borrowed directly from the EPG exercise – which South Africa would have to meet before sanctions could be lifted." (326) These Washington moves "had the effect of undermining the British diplomatic effort and increasing the pressure on the Thatcher government to impose sanctions itself." (Byrd 1988, 24)

The final years of Reagan's presidency were engulfed in scandal, and while he emerged with his popularity relatively intact, it fell to his successor, President Bush, to enforce the sanctions more fully. Thatcher's relationship with Bush never approached the kind of rapport she had had with Reagan.

17 THATCHER AGAINST THE WORLD

With Reagan's support curtailed due to Congressional action and Kohl's support never secure, by the end of 1986 forward on the issue of South Africa, it looked increasingly like it was Margaret Thatcher standing apart from all others.(Cradock 1997, 148) "Thatcher also discovered that being alone, if you happen to be the leader of a wealthy country of nearly 60 million people with a strong military tradition, was not necessarily a bad thing in an international system which remains in its essential respects anarchical." (Sharp 2003, 265-6) That Thatcher could feel that isolation was apparent from her autobiography.

"No one had a better opportunity – or a more thankless task – than I did in resolving an issue which had poisoned the West's relations with black Africa, left isolated the most advanced economic power in that continent and been used, incidentally to justify more hypocrisy and hyperbole than I heard on any other subject."(Thatcher 1993, 487) Those around her also recognized this as a tense time for her. "What stood out was her feverish and at times devious resistance to a development she was powerless to stop, and her isolation in trying to do so." (Urban 1996, 100) According to Bulpitt (1988), "Increasingly, British foreign policy was presented as the policies of one woman, so that in many respects this method became the message." (194)

Thatcher looked for alternatives to Botha and to sanctions. She had a brief hope in a black leader other than Mandela and ANC leaders, Mangosuthu Buthelezi. "Buthelezi increasingly distanced himself from the ANC and UDF as he attempted to forge an image as a moderate leader with a national constituency. His stance against armed struggle, sanctions and socialism won considerable support from the government, from liberal business leaders, and internationally. For conservative Western leaders like Margaret Thatcher in Britain, he offered the first credible alternative to the ANC." (Beinart 2001, 267) However, Buthelezi had neither the internal clout nor the international stature to be a change factor.

Increasingly, she was at odds even with her own Foreign Secretary, Geoffrey Howe. "Mrs Thatcher faced discontent among her own senior ministers over South Africa. Geoffrey Howe, in particular, found her attitude to the subject, her way of doing business and her treatment of him increasingly disagreeable. Against this, she had only the genuine but *sotto voce* support of Ronald Reagan and Helmut Kohl."(Moore 2015, 569) Thatcher was certain of the clarity of her views; she felt that others "exploded with indignation at the intrusion of fact upon rhetoric."(Thatcher 1993, 524) But she hers was an increasingly minority voice. "While Mrs Thatcher could claim to be acting rationally, with the western supporters of sanctions behaving hypocritically, her approach was out of tune with world opinion most of the time, both in the Commonwealth and in the US outside the Reagan White House." (Riddle 1991, 197)

In many cases, the iron in the Iron Lady hardened against resistance. South Africa was perhaps the primary case of this. After the EPG mission, Ramphal said, "Sanctions and peace for South Africa have now become one and the same."(Barber 1988, 111) As Filby (2015) writes, by the mid-1980s, "the issue of sanctions…had assumed an ethical mantle on which there could be no compromise." (294) Geoffrey Howe (1995) wrote in his memoirs, "Even those who agreed with us about sanctions were worried that the ferocity of our opposition to them prompted many to see us as the sole defender of apartheid." (489) There was a taint to being associated with South Africa, and increasingly with anything that touched on Thatcher's connection. "Political elites in the West…quickly realized that open identification with white South Africa could only lead to 'guilt by association'." (Tinker 1977, 132) This guilt by association was beginning to extend to Thatcher. Edwina Currie, a minister under Thatcher and

Major, observed, "it was as though she was more opposed to sanctions than to apartheid." (Palmer 2015, 169) Other advisors would not go so far. "In his memoirs, Geoffrey Howe seems to suggest that Mrs Thatcher lacked a real sense of the human suffering and humiliation it involved. But in fact her condemnation was throughout unqualified and sincere. What was at issue within Britain and between Britain and the Commonwealth partners was the most effective means for the removal of apartheid."(Cradock 1997, 145)

But Thatcher's style often got in the way. "On South Africa, the government's analysis was sound and the recoil from the emotional anti-apartheid crusade intellectually respectable. But the points were made with unnecessary acerbity." (Cradock 1997, 205) Howe (1995) agrees: "Margaret's style of argument was incorrigibly calculated to provoke the rest." (482) Thatcher felt both indignation at the hypocrisy of others; for example, "socialist France, though favouring sanctions, secretly provided the engines for combat aircraft sold to South Africa. Britain did not sell equivalent materiel or weapons." (Moore 2016, 550) Also, many advocated sanctions who had nothing at stake: "These measures were most strongly advocated by those who were most offended by white racism and those who either did not care about, or would be least affected by, their immediate consequences." (Sharp 1997, 227) She felt that there were many forms of oppression that were just as bad as apartheid, but that the racial issue made this situation seem worse. "It was this which made it possible for South Africa to receive so much attention in a world replete with odious regimes and, indeed, made it possible for several of these regimes, which mistreated their own people on a no less discriminatory basis, to assume a position of moral ascendancy in the campaign for sanctions." (Sharp 1997, 232) But she maintained that sanctions would not help, and that someone needed to keep the lines of communication open. "She felt that reform could only come from within South Africa itself, and that, when it did, the South African government would see in her a trustworthy external interlocutor who could help it move forward." (Moore 2016, 551) Her own tenure in office would not last long enough for her to be effective for long in role of honest broker.

18 INTERNAL CHANGES IN SOUTH AFRICA

In 1976, the United Nations, which over decades had progressively isolated South Africa, passed ten General Assembly resolutions against South Africa, which included one that stated that the black population "have no alternative but to resort to armed struggle to achieve their rights." (Tinker 1977, 126) In 1983, South Africa introduced some changes with a new constitution. It included votes and representation for Coloured and Indians, and supported a kind of autonomy for blacks. "Although most international and internal black reaction to the changes was hostile, the British government gave them a cautious welcome."

(Moore 2016, 548) P.W. Botha's own words had been "adapt or die," and he was at one time presented as a reformer. (Moore 2016, 549) However, the reforms also strengthened the centralized power of the white minority in power, and the office of the presidency in particular. Also, apartheid showed little chance of changing. "The pace of internal political movement within South Africa is undoubtedly determined by the conflicting pressures of the domestic political scene." (Salmon, 2017, 55) There was also the Oppenheimer thesis, which held that "apartheid survives because of slow economic growth."[13](Barber and Hill 1983, 92) One of Thatcher's beliefs was that faster growth would shift the society toward a more class-based and less race-based society, which was also held by some internal to South Africa, including perhaps Botha himself. (Salmon 56, 2017)

Often those outside South Africa failed to notice that, having grown used to criticism and

---

[13] Named for Harry Oppenheimer, who was chair of De Beers Consolidated Mines and the Anglo-American Corporation until the early 1980s.

sanctions, the South Africans had become adaptable. "The force of world opinion was not enough to induce South Africa to modify its policies designed to create apartheid between whites and non-whites." (Tinker 1977, 111) Sanctions often happened piece-meal and slowly enough that the economy was able to adapt. "Commercially, they obliged South African enterprises to redirect their business away from Britain and the United States and towards West Germany and Japan, but this search for new markets was in itself no bad thing and with the aid of subtle and not so subtle evasions of the obstacles imposed by sanctions South African trade suffered no serious net loss." (Calvocoressi 2013, 639) This was part of why Thatcher distrusted sanctions as an effective policy. Even those who advocated sanctions were unsure of their effectiveness – for example, Tutu "was an advocate of sanctions only because he could see no alternative." (Renwick 2015, 46)

However, many inside South Africa were aware that there was the possibility of change, and that it might not go well for the white minority.

According to Clark and Worger (2016), President Botha began to sell off different state-owned properties, industries and utilities to try to prevent a future black government from taking control of things that would now be in the hands of white ownership. (93-97) As Fraser and Ramphal (1986) noted, "All governments have coercive powers, and regard the maintenance of law and order as their first duty. …But the situation in South Africa is different; the objectives of the South African government are different; and the rules and conventions governing the use of state power are different." (48)

Outside and inside, different constituencies moved according to different forces. "A series of external clocks were ticking: in the Congress, in the diplomatic networks of the Commonwealth and the European Community, and in the boardrooms of U.S. corporations caught up in the pressures from shareholders, state and local governments, universities, institutional investors…. These clocks paid no attention to Southern African time; they were set to foreign time and political imperatives." (Crocker 1994, 306) In South Africa, however, there was a recognition that there were limits to the adaptability and the ability to maintain order. "The state of emergency was lifted while we [the Eminent Persons Group] were in the country on 7 March 1986, to no noticeable effect." (Fraser and Ramphal 1986, 62) In 1987, "Margaret Thatcher agreed that, while we should continue to defend our economic interests, we should never put ourselves in the position of appearing to expect, still less to rely on, the present South African government to do the right thing. They were far more likely to do the wrong thing."(Renwick 2015, 30) Renwick (2015) reminded Pik Botha of the outcome of Rhodesia, whose white leadership had held out so long that the final settlement came about in a way that effectively sidelined them, and that that principle didn't only apply to Rhodesia. (22) Meanwhile, by 1988, figures such as Niel Barnard, head of the powerful National Intelligence Service, was ready to admit, "Mandela…could not be allowed to die in jail. P.W. Botha was old-fashioned and out of touch." (Renwick 2015, 66)

Ultimately, the toll that pressure and sanctions, and in particular, the capital flight and bans on foreign investment, pushed the white business leadership to seek a more long-term, stable course of action.[14] The economy suffered a downturn, as did much of the Western economy, but could not rely on external help for support, and seemed to have reached the limits of adaptability while maintaining reasonable growth. "Psychologically, the shock sharpened fears for the future which had political repercussions, first among financiers and industrialists and so among politicians forced to face the fact that the white business community needed to participate in the world economy and feared isolation." (Calvocoressi 2013, 639) With the majority of the white community abandoning the old party line, the pace of change began to quicken in the National Party and the government. "Eventually external and internal political pressures brought the South

---

[14] In a response in Prime Minister's Question Time, 6 June 1985, Thatcher said, "It remains our view that sanctions and disinvestment will not bring about the changes that we all wish to see in South Africa." (Hansard) However, by the late 1980s, the situation seemed to have changed internally to South Africa, such that disinvestment and capital flight was exactly the mechanism that brought the business community on board with change.

African economy to its knees. Within the ruling Nationalist Party there was growing recognition that it had become necessary to bring the black majority into the political process. In 1989, F.W. de Klerk became president. De Klerk realized that apartheid had to go, and courageously he took steps to get rid of an unsustainable system."(Reitan 2003, 115) As Ramphal (1986) had noted, as long as the government was pandering to right-wing extremist fears and demands, there would be no change. (135)

As noted early, F.W. de Klerk seemed an unlikely reformer. But he was the Gorbachev-esque figure Thatcher had been waiting for; his willingness to work with Mandela made a significant difference in the peaceful transition and elimination of apartheid. "Working together, de Klerk and Mandela kept a volatile situation under control until the work was complete." (Reitan 2003, 115-6)

19 THATCHER AND MANDELA

Due to his imprisonment and with strong restrictions on who could visit and when, Nelson Mandela did not meet Margaret Thatcher until very late, in July 1990, just months before the end of her time as Prime Minister. But the two certainly knew of each other. Thatcher had an initial mistrust of Mandela, as she thought the ANC was socialist, perhaps communist, in politics and terrorist in action. (Smith 2010) However, it is also the case that Thatcher took more note of him than her predecessors had. "Nelson Mandela had been imprisoned since 1963, but Mrs Thatcher seems to have been the first British prime minister to request the South African government to release him. (Moore 2016, 550) Thatcher's rhetoric about him toned down over time. "In spite of constant government attempts to label both Winnie and Nelson Mandela as terrorists and communists, few outside white South African circles are deceived by this." (Harrison 1985, 169) Indeed, despite the different in politics, with regard to both of the Mandelas, Thatcher's reaction was clear; Nelson Mandela's imprisonment and Winnie Mandela's restricted life "underline the unacceptable nature of apartheid and the abuses of human rights connected with it."(Moore 2016, 552) Thatcher's statement to the Commons underlines this: "The Council [CHOGM] called for the opening without delay of negotiation between the South African Government and leaders of the black people in South Africa. To make such a dialogue possible, it called on the South African Government unconditionally to release Nelson Mandela and other political prisoners and to lift the ban on the African National Congress and other political parties." (Hansard, 1 July 1986)

Cradock (1997) and Renwick (2013) both report that President Botha had varying levels of contact with Mandela, often covert. Thatcher followed suit, though indirectly. "Mrs Thatcher was hearing from intelligence sources that the South African government had talked directly to Mandela about his possible release. Despite her refusal personally to talk to the ANC so long as it espoused violence, she was perfectly happy that MI6 should do so secretly outside South Africa itself – in Lusaka, for instance, and in London." (Moore 2016, 562)

Upon his release, he visited London in April 1990, and wanted to meet with Thatcher at that point.[15] Their meeting did not take place, however, until July. From her autobiography, Thatcher (1993) recounted, "Our relationship was unharmed by my straight talking. In spite of his socialist

---

[15] At first, it was thought that the lack of a meeting in April might have been due to some enmity felt on Mandela's part. However, it seems to be more simple scheduling issues. Smith (2010) in his article for *The Guardian* wrote, "Sisulu, who had been seconded to work as Mandela's appointments secretary, had 'drawn fire' from the rank and file for his handling of the liberation hero's schedule. US embassy officials were frustrated by the 'notoriously unreliable' way that Sisulu managed Mandela's diary." Andrew Harding, writing for the BBC at the time of Thatcher's death in 2013, confirms from one of Mandela's fellow prisoners that Mandela harbored no hard feelings toward her, and it was not meant as a snub.

outlook, I believed that South Africa was lucky to have a man of Mr Mandela's stature at such a time." (533) For his part, Mandela was eager to win Thatcher over, in spite of the resistance of many of colleagues in the ANC. "The rest of the ANC held against Margaret Thatcher her opposition to further sanctions. They wanted to fight with her. Mandela held the opposite view. She was, he said, a very powerful lady, 'one I would much rather have on my side'."(Renwick 2013, 196) It would seem she was won over to him, to an extent.[16] As Renwick (2015) states, she found him "supremely courteous, with a genuine nobility of bearing and – most remarkable after all that he had suffered – without any bitterness. I warmed to him." (142) This admiration did not come at the expense of her admiration for de Klerk, however, in whom she still placed the greater hope, given that he was in control of the government of South Africa for the remainder of her time as prime

---

[16] Ambassador Renwick would later tell *The Telegraph*, "Afterward, Mandela told me that the prime minister was a 'woman he could do business with'." (Renwick 11 February 2015) This parallels Thatcher's own hope, in words that she used famously with reference to Gorbachev.

minister. At the end of term in office, as she was handing over the reigns to John Major, "Mandela gave an interview about her to the BBC. In it he said that while they had disagreed about strategy, in particular about sanctions, 'we have much to be thankful for in her'."(Renwick 2015, 150).

20 THATCHER AND APARTHEID
AT THE END

Circumstances in the world were changing fast by the time Thatcher's prime ministerial career had ended. The Cold War was ending more rapidly than anyone had expected, with the fall of the Berlin Wall, the collapse of the Warsaw Pact and then of the USSR itself, and German reunification all taking place at breakneck speed, and with much more positive results than many analysts and commentators had anticipated. The same was true for South Africa. "Mrs Thatcher received from the Cabinet's policy group on South Africa (MISC 118). It calibrated the different possibilities twenty years on. It put deterioration leading to a long-drawn-out civil war at 55 per cent, the breakdown of central government and 'black revolutionary takeover' at 10 per cent, and 'peaceful transition to black majority rule' at 'perhaps 5 per cent'."(Moore 2016, 565-6) As Cradock (1997) notes, "South Africa proved to be one of those rare cases in international affairs, a story with an unexpectedly happy ending." (144)

Thatcher was not shy about taking her share of the credit for the situation. "In South Africa as 1990 opened the movement which I had hoped and worked for began. There were indications that Nelson Mandela would, after all the years of pressure, not least from me, shortly be released." (Thatcher 1993, 531) And yet, there were some who saw her influence as ineffective or negligible. Riddle, writing in 1991 just at the conclusion of Thatcher's term and the dismantling of apartheid proceeding, "Indeed, while her policy gave her some standing with the Pretoria regime, it was not an influence which produced any apparent results." (198) The *New Statesman*, a paper admittedly biased against Thatcher, was more scathing – "Thatcher, it was said – no doubt to her chagrin – had contributed nothing to the change." (Hyam and

Henshaw 2007, 337) This is probably over the top. After all, as Barber (1988) pointed out, "Pretoria has attempted to retain good relations with London and there is respect for Mrs Thatcher as a forceful, determined leader, both because of the influence she carries among other Western leaders and because of her firm opposition to sanctions against the Republic." (102)

The question of Thatcher's influence parallels the question of influence of others, also. "As important as the AAM and the Church were in opposing apartheid, it was internal events within South Africa as well as the end of the Cold War (specifically the settlement of Namibia and Angola in 1989) that ensured the regime's demise." (Filby 2015, 296) Even as Britain had a leading role in trade and history, by the end of apartheid, Britain's importance had slipped; during the 1980s, it was already seen, "for Britain, relations with South Africa can no longer be seen predominantly in bilateral terms; they are firmly caught up in its relations with other Western states." (Barber and Hill 1983, 24)

The internal changes were the key changes. They were interpreted differently. Papenfus (2011) gives credit to ministers like Pik Botha, seeing the changes coming: "Pik Botha's controversial vision of 1986 had become a reality. The next day would see the inauguration of a black president, as Pik had predicted in the dark apartheid years. And he was to serve under that black president, in his cabinet." (749)   But much rested on the transformation of thinking of F.W. de Klerk, which seemed less likely to be influenced by Thatcher or other outside forces, as much as it was a change from within. "But the main sources of de Klerk's conversion lay nearer home, in his religious convictions, his commitment to civil, as opposed to military, government, in his awareness of South Africa's isolation, its serious financial crisis and, above all, the sterility of apartheid." (Cradock 1997, 154-5) Thatcher recognized this change as a positive one, and worked to support it, interpreting it as a confirmation. "The de Klerk *deus ex machina* transformed the arguments over apartheid. The British strategy was vindicated. Beleaguered British delegations in international gatherings saw relief at hand."(Cradock 1997, 155)

By this time, however, internal politics in Westminster had caught up with Thatcher. Her hard line approach was wearing thin on the electorate and her Parliamentary colleagues. "Her qualities of courage and determination made her outstanding, but beyond a point they were self-defeating." (Biffen 2013, 424) For over a decade, she had been Prime Minister, a long enough time to see most of her original team of loyal supporters depart in one fashion or another, many near the end in unhappy circumstances. In the end, the primary force behind her departure was her beleaguered Foreign Secretary (later, Deputy Prime Minister and Leader of the House, high sounding but somewhat meaningless appointments) Geoffrey Howe. "Geoffrey Howe, one of the most outstandingly capable members of the government led by Thatcher, finally lost patience with her increasing belief that she alone knew best and, with his resignation speech in the House of Commons, precipitated her downfall in November 1990." (Brown 2013, 97) Gaskarth (2013) confirms this assessment, that Howe's resignation and speech "was a catalyst for rebellion that ended Thatcher's leadership." (15) She would visit post-apartheid South Africa, but only as a former prime minister.

21 CONCLUSION

From her earliest public statements, it was clear that Margaret Thatcher held strong disapproval for apartheid. "'I loathe apartheid and everything connected with it,' she had said in a speech to the National Press Club in Australia in 1979." (Filby 2015, 292) Hers was more than a disgust for racism, but had deeper ideological grounds. "There is no doubt, however, that Mrs Thatcher thought that apartheid was unjust – a form of oppressive 'radical socialism' which forcibly moved people hither and thither, kept them poor and denied their human worth and their right to vote." (Moore 2016, 545) Thatcher was accused of being racist by Commonwealth colleagues, by South African ministers, and by the press, but the issue of racism is a larger one than apartheid. "For outside of places such as South Africa, racism is not an officially proclaimed ideology; it is almost unconscious." (Tinker 1977, 73) But perhaps the statement of Nelson Mandela might provide a final word of her view of apartheid: "Her credentials in this regard were confirmed by no less a person than Nelson Mandela after he met her in the summer of 1990. 'There is no doubt', he said '…that she is an enemy of apartheid'." (Sharp 1997, 228)

So, did Thatcher do the right thing, but in the wrong way? Ian Gilmour (1992), Defence Minister under Heath and one of Thatcher's original Cabinet, wrote, "The perennial cause of rows with the Commonwealth was the treatment of South Africa and the question of sanctions. Initially I had a good deal of sympathy for Mrs Thatcher's opposition to mandatory sanctions being imposed on South Africa. I was very doubtful that they would be economically effective, feared that they would make the Afrikaaners still more intransigent, and anticipated that they would be a potent cause of increased misery to much of the black population." (259) However, Gilmour was to later change his mind on the subject: "The evidence suggests, however, that all those fears were mistaken. Sanctions and economic pressure turned out to be strikingly effective in converting South Africa's leaders to the need for reform." (259) The issue of sanctions swirled through the relations with the Commonwealth and other nations, and in the end, it was foreign capital issues that seemed to have the most impact on the white business community. David Cameron, who would go on to be Conservative Prime Minister, was quoted in *The Observer* and *The Independent* in 2006 as saying that "Mr Mandela was 'one of the greatest men alive'. He said, 'The mistakes my party made in the past with respect to relations with the ANC and sanctions on South Africa made it all the more important to listen now'." (Woolf 2006)

Perhaps in addition to Thatcher's concern about sanctions not being effective because too many nations would find ways around them, there was a bit of self-fulfilling prophecy. The usefulness of sanctions could easily be render moot given "their implementation would rest with those who are the most skeptical about their desirability and effectiveness." (Barber and Hill 1983, 96) Would Thatcher have enforced sanctions? The Reagan administration, having had a veto override on the issue, was nonetheless less than diligent at enforcing the legislation; it fell to his successor to toughen the enforcement, which was quickly followed with the shift in thinking and action in South Africa. But it is difficult to gauge if Thatcher's read on P.W. Botha, being different from F.W. de Klerk, was the correct one; Botha seemed more impervious to outside pressure or influence, and much more likely to entrench in response. Perhaps Thatcher, being someone of a similar type, recognized this in Botha.

As Gilmour (1992) continued, "Even if, however, the anti-sanctions argument had been wholly correct, the way it was presented and the manner in which the government handled the Commonwealth would not have gained applause. An association of largely non-white countries was bound to feel strongly about apartheid, but the British Prime Minister never seemed to take proper account of their sensitivities." (259) Her fervor for anti-sanctions was never seen to be matched by her fervor for anti-apartheid, despite speeches and statements that were clear. Riddle (1991), states, "She appeared not to appreciate the need at times for symbolic actions, albeit ineffective ones. Thus, by seeking consistency and being impatient with diplomatic gestures, Mrs Thatcher alienated large sections of Third World opinion which accused her of appeasing apartheid." (198) Her attitudes toward South Africa, toward the Commonwealth, toward the Foreign Office, and toward the rest of world were perhaps highlighted most sharply on this issue. "Thatcher's predisposition and its consequences were no more in evidence than on the question of the part international society should attempt to play in ending apartheid in South Africa." (Sharp 1997, 226-7)

That is not to say that these were good qualities. Brown (2013) states, "Her foreign policy instincts were far from uniformly impressive. During the years of Nelson Mandela's incarceration in Robben Island prison, she was more sympathetic to the South African apartheid regime than to Mandela." (Brown 2013, 97) Sharp (1997) follows up, stating, without placing a particular value judgment, "Indeed, if influence means having a concrete effect on outcomes rather than just participating and being seen to participate, then British influence in the postwar Commonwealth was never greater than under Thatcher's prime ministership." (234)   Influence was certain, but often as an agitator or thwarter, like a chess piece that isn't moved, but seems to block all other possible moves. "Opinions differ as to whether this was one of the more elevated episodes in postwar British diplomacy." (Sharp 1997, 234)

Percy Cradock, senior foreign policy advisor to Thatcher, stated, "our contribution was unique, but its effect should not be exaggerated." (Cradock 1997, 158) On the other hand, in his tribute to her at the time of her death, F.W. de Klerk said "she exerted more influence on what happened in South Africa than any other political leader."(Renwick 2015, 7)   Mandela also acknowledged her contribution, but there is an air of diplomatic courtesy about it: "As Mandela publicly acknowledged when Margaret Thatcher visited the country after her resignation, 'We have a good deal to thank her for.' But external pressures, whether from Washington or London, were not decisive. The crucial factor was the emergence of an enlightened and courageous South African leader."(Cradock 1997, 157)

Even if Thatcher did the right thing in terms of holding firm to the policy of anti-sanctions through time as Prime Minister, her manner did not help her cause, or significantly affect the development of a post-apartheid society in South Africa. As Ramsbotham (2009) states, whatever her public stance towards issues, Thatcher was typically pragmatic. That pragmatism seemed to be missing here. While Thatcher herself celebrated her "vindication" in her autobiography, and several key advisors also continue the line that anti-sanctions was the proper way to go in their subsequent writings, almost all also acknowledge, from Howe on down, that the tone of her words and actions spoke volumes beyond what she was actually saying. What she termed "straight talk" in her autobiography in fact often came across in a more combative and sometimes condescending way. (Thatcher 1993, 553) Her wish to be the "guiding star" never came about; can one be considered a leader if there are no followers? (Moore 2016, 555)

When Thatcher and Mandela both passed away in 2013, while Thatcher was honored at her funeral, it was Mandela who was celebrated much more widely around the world.[17] Thatcher is remembered with regard to her role in the conflicts over South Africa not so much as one who succeeded or failed, but rather by the tone of how she spoke and acted, and in that regard, she did nothing to lessen conflict. Upon taking office, on the steps of No. 10 Downing Street, Thatcher quoted a prayer from St. Francis of Assisi, which began with the verse, "Where there is discord, may we bring harmony." (Thatcher 1979) If judged by this standard, with regard to South Africa, Thatcher had failed.

---

[17] One of the honors accorded to Thatcher at her funeral was attendance of the Queen, who had only attended in her six decades on the throne one other Prime Minister's funeral – that of Winston Churchill. The reasoning behind Her Majesty's decision to pay tribute to Thatcher has been speculated, but never officially explained.

22 BIBLIOGRAPHY

Ashford, Nicholas. "Thatcher refuses to budge over sanctions." *The Times,* 21 October 1985. http://www.margaretthatcher.org/document/111649

Barber, James P., and Christopher R Hill. *The Uneasy Relationship.* London: Heinemann for the Royal Institute of International Affairs, 1983.

Barber, James P. "Southern Africa," in *British Foreign Policy under Thatcher,* edited by Peter Byrd, 99-121. Oxford: Philip Allan, 1988.

Bartlett, C.J. *British Foreign Policy in the Twentieth Century.* British History in Perspective Series. London: Macmillan, 1989.

Beinart, William. *Twentieth-Century South Africa.* Oxford: Oxford University Press, 2001.

Berlinski, Carol. *"There is No Alternative." Why Margaret Thatcher Matters.* New York: Basic Books, 2008.

Biffen, John. *Semi-Detached.* London: Biteback Books, 2013.

Brickley, Carol, Terry O'Halloran, and David Reed. *South Africa: Britain out of Apartheid, Apartheid out of Britain.* London: Larkin Publications, 1985.

Brown, Archie. *The Myth of the Strong Leader: Political Leadership in the Modern Age.* New York: Basic Books, 2013. (Advance proof copy)

Buller, Jim. "Foreign and Defence Policy under Thatcher and Major." *Contemporary British Conservatism,* Steve Ludlam and Martin Smith, eds. New York: St. Martin's Press, 1996.

Bulpitt, James. "Rational Politicians and Conservative Statecraft in the Open Polity," in *British Foreign Policy under Thatcher,* edited by Peter Byrd, 214-256. Oxford: Philip Allan, 1988.

Byrd, Peter, ed. *British Foreign Policy under Thatcher.* Oxford: Philip Allan, 1988.

Calvocoressi, Peter. *World Politics Since 1945.* New York: Routledge, 2013.

Carrington, Peter. *Reflecting on Things Past: The Memoirs of Peter Lord Carrington.* New York: Harper & Row, 1989.

Clark, Nancy L., and William H. Worger, eds. *South Africa: The Rise and Fall of Apartheid.* London: Routledge, 2016.

Cradock, Percy. *In Pursuit of British Interests: Reflections on Foreign Policy under Margaret Thatcher and John Major.* London: John Murray, 1997.

Crocker, Chester A, and George P Shultz. *High Noon In Southern Africa.* Johannesburg: Jonathan Ball Publishers, 1994.

Dale, Iain, ed. *Margaret Thatcher in her Own Words*. London: Biteback Books, 2010.

Doxey, Margaret P. *International Sanctions in Contemporary Perspective*. New York: St Martin's Press, 1996.

The Economist, 19 October 1985

Elliott, Claire. "Queen 'so enraged' by Thatcher on South Africa's apartheid." *Daily Mail*.28 December 2017. http://www.dailymail.co.uk/news/article-5219155/Queen-enraged-Thatcher-apartheid.htlm

Evans, Eric J. *Thatcher and Thatcherism,* 3rd ed. London: Routledge, 2013.

Filby, Eliza. *God & Mrs Thatcher: The Battle for Britain's Soul.* London: Biteback Books, 2015

Fraser, Malcolm, and Shridath Ramphal. *Mission to South Africa: The Commonwealth Report*. Hammondsworth: Penguin Books for the Commonwealth Secretariat, 1986.

Gamble, Andrew. *The Free Economy and the Strong State: The Politics of Thatcherism*. Durham, NC: Duke University Press, 1988;.

Gaskarth, Jamie. *British Foreign Policy.* Cambridge: Polity Press, 2013.

Gilmour, Ian. *Dancing with Dogma: Britain under Thatcherism*. London: Simon & Schuster, 1992.

Hansard, Prime Minister's Question Time, 6 June 1985.
http://hansard.millbanksystems.com/commons/1
985/jun/06/engagements#S6CV0080P0_198506
06_HOC_141

Hansard, Prime Minister's Question Time, 17 June
1986.
http://hansard.millbanksystems.com/commons/1
986/jun/17/engagements#S6CV0099P0_198606
17_HOC_136

Hansard, Prime Minister's Question Time, 19 June
1986.
http://hansard.millbanksystems.com/commons/1
986/jun/19/engagements#S6CV0099P0_198606
19_HOC_128

Hansard, Prime Minister's Question Time. 1 July 1986.
http://hansard.millbanksystems.com/commons/1
986/jul/01/engagements#S6CV0100P0_198607
01_HOC_127

Hansard, Statement on the Commonwealth Head of
Government Meeting, 22 October 1987.
http://hansard.millbanksystems.com/commons/1
987/oct/22/commonwealth-heads-of-
government-
meeting#S6CV0120P0_19871022_HOC_194

Hansard, Statement on the Commonwealth Head of
Government Meeting, 26 October 1989.
http://hansard.millbanksystems.com/commons/1
989/oct/26/commonwealth-
conference#S6CV0158P0_19891026_HOC_213

Hansard, Statement on the European Council, 1 July
     1986.
     http://hansard.millbanksystems.com/commons/1
     986/jul/01/european-
     council#S6CV0100P0_19860701_HOC_197

Hansard, Statement on the Falklands, 26 April 1982.
     http://hansard.millbanksystems.com/commons/1
     982/apr/26/falkland-
     islands#S6CV0022P0_19820426_HOC_194

Hansard, Written Answers, 16 April 1986.
     http://hansard.millbanksystems.com/written_ans
     wers/1986/apr/16/libya-trade-
     sanctions#S6CV0095P0_19860416_CWA_66

Hansard, Written Answers, 12 January 1987.
     http://hansard.millbanksystems.com/written_ans
     wers/1987/jan/12/south-africa-
     sanctions#S6CV0108P0_19870112_CWA_15

Harding, Andrew.   "Thatcher's role 'in saving Nelson
     Mandela'." BBC, 8 April, 2013.
     http://www.bbc.com/news/world-africa-
     22069896

Harris, Robin, ed. *Margaret Thatcher: The Collected
     Speeches*. New York: HarperCollins, 1997.

Harrison, Nancy. *Winnie Mandela: Mother of a
     Nation*. London: Victor Gollancz Ltd, 1985.

Henderson, David. "The Problem with Sanctions." Library of Economics and Liberty. 21 December 2009. http://econlog.econlib.org/archives/2009/12/the_problem_wit_1.html

Howe, Geoffrey. *Conflict of Loyalty*. London: Palgrave Macmillan, 1995.

Hyam, Ronald, and Peter Henshaw. *The Lion And The Springbok*. Cambridge: Cambridge University Press, 2007.

Jeffries, Stuart. "Game of thrones: behind closed doors with Margaret Thatcher and the Queen." *The Guardian,* 25 September 2013. https://www.theguardian.com/stage/2013/sep/25/handbagged-queen-margaret-thatcher

Jenkins, Simon. *Thatcher and Sons: A Revolution in Three Acts*. London: Allen Lane/Penguin, 2006.

Letwin, Shirley Robin. *The Anatomy of Thatcherism*. New Brunswick: Transaction Publishers, 1992.

Ludlam, Steve and Martin J. Smith, eds. *Contemporary British Conservatism*. London: Macmillan, 1996.

"Margaret Thatcher Foundation." Margaretthatcher.org (accessed October 10, 2017).

Moore, Charles. *Margaret Thatcher: At her zenith: In London, Washington and Moscow*. New York: Alfred Knopf, 2016.

Morgan, Kenneth O. *Twentieth-Century Britain.*
Oxford: Oxford University Press, 2005.

Neil, Andrew. *Full disclosure*. London: Pan, 1997.

O'Sullivan, John. *The President, the Pope, and the
Prime Minister: Three Who Changed the World.*
Washington, DC: Regnery Publishing, 2016.

Otte, T.G., ed. *The Makers of British Foreign Policy:
From Pitt to Thatcher.* Basingstoke: Palgrave,
2003.

Pal, L. "Case study method and policy analysis."
*Thinking Like a Policy Analyst: Policy Analysis
as a Clinical Profession.* New York: Palgrave
Macmillan US, 2005.

Palmer, Dean. *The Queen and Mrs Thatcher: An
Inconvenient Relationship.* Stroud,
Gloucestershire: The History Press, 2015.

Papenfus, Theresa, and Sandra Mills. *Pik Botha And
His Times*. Pretoria: Litera, 2011.

Preeg, Ernest H. *Trade Policy Ahead: Three Tracks and
One Question.* Washington, DC: Center for
Strategic & International Studies, 1995.

Pruit, Dean G., and Sung Hee Kim. *Social Conflict:
Escalation, Stalemate, and Settlement.* 3rd ed.
Boston: McGraw-Hill, 2004.

Ramsbotham, Oliver, Tom Woodhouse, and Hugh Miall. *Contemporary Conflict Resolution: The prevention, management and transformation of deadly conflicts*. 2nd ed. Cambridge: Polity Press, 2009.

Reitan, E.A. *The Thatcher Revolution: Margaret Thatcher, John Major, Tony Blair, and the Transformation of Modern Britain, 1979-2001*. Oxford: Rowman & Littlefield Publishers, Ltd, 2003.

Renwick, Robin. *A Journey with Margaret Thatcher: Foreign Policy under the Iron Lady*. London: Biteback Books, 2013.

Renwick, Robin, *The End of Apartheid*. London: Biteback Books, 2015.

Renwick, Robin. "Margaret Thatcher's secret campaign to end apartheid." *The Telegraph*, 11 February 2015. http://www.telegraph.co.uk/news/politics/marga ret-thatcher/11403728/Margaret-Thatchers-secret-campaign-to-end-apartheid.html

Renwick, Robin. *Unconventional Diplomacy in South Africa*. New York: St. Martin's Press, 1997.

Riddle, Peter. *The Thatcher Era and Its Legacy*. Oxford: Blackwell Press, 1991.

Robbins, Carla Anne. "Why Economic Sanctions Rarely Work." *Bloomberg Business Week.* 24 May 2013. https://www.bloomberg.com/news/articles/2013-05-23/why-economic-sanctions-rarely-work

Salmon, Patrick. *The Challenges of Apartheid: UK-South African Relations, 1985-86.* Documents on British Policy Overseas, Series III, Volume IX. New York: Whitehall History Publishing/ Routledge, 2017.

Sampson, Anthony. *Black and Gold: Tycoons, Revolutionaries and Apartheid.* London: Hodder & Stoughton, 1987.

Sampson, Anthony. *Mandela: The Authorised Biography.* New York: Harper Press, 1999.

Sharp, Paul. "British Foreign Policy under Margaret Thatcher," in *The Makers of British Foreign Policy: From Pitt to Thatcher,* edited by T.G. Otte, 261-288. Basingstoke: Palgrave, 2003.

Sharp, Paul. *Thatcher's Diplomacy: The Revival of British Foreign Policy.* London: Macmillan Press, 1997.

Simons, Margaret, and Malcolm Fraser. *Malcolm Fraser.* Carlton, Vic.: Melbourne University Publishing, 2009.

Smith, David. "Nelson Mandela and Margaret
     Thatcher: The meeting that never was." *The
     Guardian,* 28 November, 2010.
     https://www.theguardian.com/world/2010/nov/2
     8/nelson-mandela-margaret-thatcher-meeting

Tayfur, M.F. "Main approaches to the study of foreign
     policy: A review." *METU Studies in
     Development* 21, no. 1: 113-141, 1994.

Taylor, Adam. "13 times that sanctions really worked."
     Washington Post, 28 April 2014.
     https://www.washingtonpost.com/news/worldvi
     ews/wp/2014/04/28/13-times-that-economic-
     sanctions-really-
     worked/?utm_term=.e8f3ebdd73c5

Thatcher, Margaret. *Margaret Thatcher: The Downing
     Street Years.* New York: HarperCollins
     Publishers, 1993.

Thatcher, Margaret. "Remarks on becoming Prime
     Minister (St Francis' prayer). 4 May 1979.
     https://www.margaretthatcher.org/document/10
     4078

Thatcher, Margaret. Speech to the College of Europe,
     20 September, 1988. In *Margaret Thatcher: In
     Her Own Words*, Iain Dale, ed. London:
     Biteback, 2010.

Thatcher, Margaret. *Statecraft: Strategies for a
     Changing World.* New York: HarperCollins
     Publishers, 2002.

Theis, C.G. "A pragmatic guide to qualitative historical analysis in the study of international relations." *International Studies Perspectives* 3: 351-372, 2002.

Tinker, Hugh. *Race, Conflict, and the International Order.* New York: St. Martin's Press, 1977.

Urban, George. *Diplomacy and Disillusion at the Court of Margaret Thatcher: An Insider's View.* London: I.B. Tauris & Co., 1996.

Vinen, Richard. *Thatcher's Britain: The Politics and Social Upheaval of the 1980s.* London: Pocket Books, 2009.

Wall, Stephen. *A Stranger in Europe: Britain and the EU from Thatcher to Blair.* Oxford: Oxford University Press, 2008.

Wapshott, Nicholas. *Ronald Reagan and Margaret Thatcher: A Political Marriage.* New York: Sentinel, 2007.

Woolf, Marie. "Cameron Apologies for Thatcher apartheid policies." *The Independent*, 26 August 2006. http://www.independent.co.uk/news/uk/politics/cameron-apologises-for-thatcher-apartheid-policies-413569.html

Yin, R.K. "The case study crisis: Some answers." *Administrative Science Quarterly* 26, no. 1: 58-65, 1981.

ABOUT THE AUTHOR

Kurt Messick worked in the House of Commons during Margaret Thatcher's tenure as Prime Minister, working as an office manager, researcher, constituency aide, election assistant, freelance speech writer, and general student of political affairs. Later in his career, after several rounds of political and public relations positions, he settled on teaching and ministry as his true vocation, while learning, reading and writing remain his strong avocation. This particular text comes out of work done with the American Military University, National Security Studies and Conflict Resolution, for which he was awarded the MA with honors in 2018 for work in this subject. He currently lives in Bloomington, Indiana.

www.ingramcontent.com/pod-product-compliance
Lightning Source LLC
Chambersburg PA
CBHW031230250726
48655CB00005B/1886

9 781727 021769